Praise for Flesh Wounds

'A new classic … a breathtaking accomplishment in style and empathy'
– Greg Sheridan, *The Australian*

'Both poignant and wildly entertaining'
– Mandy Sayer, *Sydney Morning Herald*

'Heartbreaking and hilarious … I couldn't put it down'
– Tracey Spicer, *Sun-Herald*

'Engrossing and extremely funny' – *The Saturday Paper*

'It is Glover's unsentimental, bemused but steady grip on reality that
makes his story so unputdownable and so strong' – Matthew Parris

Praise for Richard Glover

'Hilarious' – Candida Baker

'An Australian Seinfeld' – Wil Anderson

'Desperately, wickedly funny' – Augusten Burroughs

'Full-on, uncontrollable, laugh-till-you-weep stories'
– Geraldine Brooks

'Glover is better than Proust. OK, maybe not better, but how
often do you find yourself in a cold bath at midnight still
chuckling over Proust.' – Debra Adelaide

Richard Glover has written a number of bestselling books, including *The Mud House, In Bed with Jocasta* and *George Clooney's Haircut and Other Cries for Help*. He writes a weekly column for the *Sydney Morning Herald* and presents the comedy program *Thank God It's Friday* on ABC Local Radio. To find out more, visit www.richardglover.com.au

Flesh Wounds

RICHARD
GLOVER

Flesh Wounds

ABC
Books

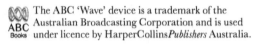 The ABC 'Wave' device is a trademark of the
Australian Broadcasting Corporation and is used
under licence by HarperCollins*Publishers* Australia.

First published in Australia in 2015
by HarperCollins*Publishers* Australia Pty Limited
ABN 36 009 913 517
harpercollins.com.au

HarperCollins*Publishers*
Level 13, 201 Elizabeth Street, Sydney NSW 2000, Australia
Unit D1, 63 Apollo Drive, Rosedale, Auckland 0632, New Zealand
A 53, Sector 57, Noida, UP, India
1 London Bridge Street, London, SE1 9GF, United Kingdom
2 Bloor Street East, 20th floor, Toronto, Ontario M4W 1A8, Canada
195 Broadway, New York NY 10007, USA

National Library of Australia Cataloguing-in-Publication entry:

Glover, Richard, author.
  Flesh wounds / Richard Glover.
  ISBN: 978 0 7333 3432 0 (paperback)
  ISBN: 978 1 4607 0502 5 (ebook : epub)
  Glover, Richard.
  Radio broadcasters – Australia – Biography.
  Authors – Australia – Biography.
A823.3

Cover design by Hazel Lam, HarperCollins Design Studio
Cover images courtesy of Richard Glover
Author photograph by Marco Del Grande (Fairfax Syndication)
Page 207 Crown Copyright image, reproduced courtesy of The National Archives,
London, England
Typeset in Baskerville MT by Kirby Jones
Printed and bound in Australia by Griffin Press
The papers used by HarperCollins in the manufacture of this book
are a natural, recyclable product made from wood grown in sustainable
plantation forests. The fibre source and manufacturing processes meet
recognised international environmental standards, and carry certification.

'Imagination was given to man to compensate him for what he is not; a sense of humour to console him for what he is.'

Sir Francis Bacon

For Dan and Joe

My father and mother on their wedding day, Lancashire, 1946.

Please start here

According to my mother, I was the first artificial insemination baby in Australia. The claim is not as unlikely as it sounds; the dates work out. She wasn't talking about IVF or test tubes, just about sperm and a turkey-baster. Old-style. So her story makes some sense. It was her reason for needing help that was strange. She and my father were having trouble conceiving, which is not surprising when you consider she'd never slept with him. Not once. They'd been married twelve years and still the marriage was unconsummated. And even in 1958, it was hard to get pregnant without having sex.

They were living in Papua New Guinea where medical facilities were scarce, so they came down to Sydney to see an infertility specialist. My father gave his sperm and my mother submitted to the procedure. And, according to my mother, it worked. She was both pregnant and a virgin. So, at this point, you may wish to call me Jesus.

My father had a different story, but only slightly different. Yes, my mother refused to sleep with him, and yes, they'd booked into an Australian hospital to see if artificial insemination could be the answer. In my father's version, though, the procedure didn't work. They went back to New Guinea and she was forced to finally have sex with him, just the once, in order to have me. I don't know which story is right. Either way, I find it hard to think of myself as a love child.

A few years later, we moved from Papua New Guinea – first to Sydney and then to Canberra. In all that time I never felt like the favourite, which is hard when you are an only child. My mother was distant, both from me and my father. She would tell anyone who listened about the unusual circumstances of my birth, as if it made the two of us a little bit posh: a child produced without recourse to rutting. Her tone was the one you'd use when your child has won a competition.

Some years on, having finished school, I travelled overseas, hoping to meet my English grandparents. By then my parents had split up – my mother moving to a country town far away. I rang her to request contact details for her side of the family. There was a disapproving sigh on her end of the phone. She wasn't in a position to put me in contact with her family. Frankly, she refused. When I asked her why, she told me a story I'd heard growing up, without ever really taking it in. It described the cause of all that followed: her hasty but loveless marriage to my father, their escape to New Guinea, and the way I'd never had any contact with my maternal grandparents.

As she explained it, she was a child from an upper-class family. Her father had always been busy with affairs of state, working with Sir Winston Churchill both before and during the war. And she – like me – had been an only child. Not properly loved, not properly wanted, and sent away to boarding school at just seven years of age. She understood, to some extent, the actions of her parents. They were from that class of people for whom boarding school was customary. But part of her could never forgive, could never forget. It was in her rush to escape the elite boarding school that she had met my father, in his smart World War II naval uniform, and then onwards to what she saw as a disastrous marriage. She didn't want me fraternising with the people who had caused all this misery.

Fair enough. So, I went to England, nineteen years old, armed with the name of my father's sister: Auntie Audrey, a school teacher in Bristol. I met her daughters, my three cousins, the first relatives I'd ever encountered. After a few days, my aunt asked whether I was planning a trip to see my mother's family, and I said, 'No, Auntie,' before rapidly repeating the tragic tale: my mother's neglectful upper-class family, the posh boarding school, handsome navy captain, loveless marriage, turkey-baster, sperm, me.

'So, Auntie, as you can see, it's not really possible for me to go and see them.'

Through all this a smile was forming on my aunt's face.

'A posh boarding school, you say?'

'Yes, Auntie.'

'Father worked with Sir Winston?'

'Yes, Auntie.'

'Would you like to see a picture of your grandparents? And your mother's sisters?'

Sisters? I thought to myself. *There were no sisters. She was an only child.*

All I said, however, was, 'Yes, I'd love to see the pictures.'

My aunt went upstairs. I could hear her rummaging around in her bedroom, opening drawers and cupboards. She came down holding a tiny black-and-white photograph. 'Here's a photo of your mother's family,' she said, handing it over.

I stared at the small image, transfixed but confused. There were five people in the photo – my mother, her two sisters and their parents. I could recognise my mother. And the others looked like her: they were clearly a family. They were also clearly northern working-class. Actually, they were northern working class as rendered by Monty Python. The father virtually had a hanky on his head.

'They look lovely,' I said.

'They were lovely,' replied my aunt. 'Your mother was ashamed of them. She wanted to be something better. She didn't even invite them to the wedding. They came anyway and stood outside in the rain, throwing confetti.'

*

My mother, my aunt explained, grew up in a cramped two-up, two-down terrace house in Lancashire, left school at fourteen and was working as a hairdresser's apprentice when she met my father, who was only a smidge further up the social hierarchy. Her dad – my grandfather – had laboured in a cotton mill; her sisters ran a boarding house. The stories about working for Sir Winston, life in the boarding school, the posh accent, even her status as an only child: all of it was invention.

I know the obvious thing to say is that this left me gutted. That I sat there sobbing, reflecting on the fact that all my life I'd been fed a lie. Or that, in response to this revelation, I reassessed my relationship to social class, deciding to celebrate my true proletarian British background by henceforth dressing in a cloth cap and shoving a ferret down my trousers.

The reality was that I hardly noticed what my aunt was saying. At nineteen, on my first trip outside Australia, I didn't really care about the social standing of my mother's parents, nor whether my mother was a poshie or a non-poshie. It all seemed rather arcane, nowhere near as interesting as the fact that my cousins were about to take me horse-riding at a farm down the road.

This lack of interest will sound weird, I know, to anyone who comes from a vaguely functional family. How can you not care about your parents and their antecedents? Maybe there'll be others, though, who'll think it sounds normal. Caring about your parents can hinge on whether they cared about you. My mother, in all the important ways, had disappeared from my life by the time I was fifteen, and even in the years she was present had been disconnected, self-interested, otherwise engaged. I'd always considered myself self-raising, like flour.

It was only years later that other questions began to press themselves forward. Can you really be self-raising, like flour? Or is that just a glib way to pretend that bad parenting doesn't hurt? Is it possible to be a good parent yourself if your own parents were not what you ordered? And is the personality of the ill-parented person, both the good parts and the bad, really nothing but scar tissue, grown around this elemental hurt?

My attitude at nineteen – 'I'm just not that interested' – may have been healthy, in a self-protective, let's-get-on-with-things way, but it was an attitude that became difficult to maintain as the years went by. And so, more than three decades on, I decided to discover where I came from.

Chapter One

This is where my memory starts: me as a self-sufficient child, distant from my parents. It was the early 1960s; my parents had just returned to Australia from New Guinea, where they'd spent twelve years helping establish a daily newspaper, the *South Pacific Post*. Both had good jobs in Sydney. My father, Ted, worked for a local publishing company and then later for the *Reader's Digest*. He was handsome, with jet-black hair swept into place with Brylcreem, rather like the Don Draper character in *Mad Men*. My mother, who called herself Bunty, worked as an arts publicist, mainly for The Australian Opera and The Australian Ballet. She was blonde, vivacious and would dress stylishly in bright designer clothes. My mother and father didn't really behave like parents to me or as partners to each other. It was more a case of two self-involved individuals who happened to rent a room to a boarder of mystifyingly modest height.

They – or rather we – lived in a two-storey house of normal size, with a circular drive squeezed into the front yard as a nod to feudal grandeur. It had a pool out the back and a long, bright sunroom for entertaining. The sunroom had a bar at one end, decorated to an Hawaiian theme. A pair of over-sized salad servers, embellished with frangipanis, was mounted on the wall behind the bar, presumably to celebrate Hawaii's famous love of salad. A glass bowl held packets of motel matches – 'Stay at the Sea-Breeze on Queensland's Gold Coast' – and there were several large lighters, embedded in lumps of marble, which I'd occasionally be required to carry around, igniting the cigarettes of guests. In this household, there'd be no problems if a visitor craved either a drink or a smoke.

My parents worked hard and enjoyed a busy social life. They'd arrive home just before dinner and then, quite often, would head to a party or the theatre, clambering their way up the social ladder, leaving me with a teenage babysitter. Or they'd host elaborate dinner parties – a clatter of music and conversation floating up the stairs towards my bedroom.

At such events, my mother spoke loudly in a posh, strangulated accent. She sounded like the Queen Mum – if the Queen Mum had been required to instruct a group of slightly deaf workmen standing on the other side of a noisy road. It wasn't only the manner of speaking, it was the words themselves – words, I now realise, which were chosen to prove her aristocratic standing. It was never a 'toilet' but always a 'lavatory'. 'I'm just off to the lavatory,' she'd announce at high volume, almost constantly, to whole roomfuls of people, so frequently that her guests must have worried about the state of her bladder. In the same spirit, it was 'napkin', not 'serviette'; 'sofa', not 'couch'; 'pudding', not 'sweet'; 'spectacles', not 'glasses'; and 'drawing room', not 'lounge'. My childhood was a blizzard of these terms, my mother never more pleased than when she could work several into a single sentence:

'Let's head into the drawing room for some pudding, if you're all sure you don't need the lavatory.'

'Leave your napkin behind; you won't need it once you're sitting on the sofa in the drawing room.'

'The lavatory is just through there, past the sofa; you'll see the way through your spectacles.'

*

When I read autobiographies I'm amazed by people's ability to recall their early childhood. The film star Diane Cilento, for example, wrote about the music teacher she had when she was eight or nine years old, and remembered everything – the teacher's name, personality, even the state of her teeth. 'Theodora Benson was a dark-haired melancholic with chipped teeth and moles all over her face.' Was Diane just making this up? Do most people retain this stuff? I try to recall my own piano teacher but can't get a picture to form, either in terms of the moles or the name. I can certainly remember the long bicycle ride to the teacher's house and the steep upwards slope just before I got there. I remember the rush of pleasure as I whooshed back down the hill at the end of the lesson. I also recall the music teacher's house, double-fronted, with a long corridor to the back room, where the piano stood. And the musty cabbagey smell of the place. And the boredom. Other than that, nothing. I can't even recall the gender of the teacher, never mind supply a detailed dental report.

When I think of my childhood it's like a broken wine bottle smashed on the floor. The memories are shards of glass, all messed up. It's impossible to know what fits where.

- A teenager comes over with his parents and sings all eighteen minutes of 'Alice's Restaurant', while strumming along on his guitar. I'm about nine or ten and I'm very impressed.
- Cicadas. Collecting them. From a tree over the road.
- A dead dog lies on the roadside. It's been hit by a car and left there, its eye hanging out.
- Me beating an upholstered pool chair with a stick, bored in the late afternoon after school, pretending I am 'teacher' and caning the pupils.
- Cycling to the home of a boy my mother wanted me to like, but I had my doubts about. He had a weird big head.

- My parents hosting a party at home and me being told to stand and read a short story for the group. It was *The Loaded Dog* by Henry Lawson. Mortifying.

- A bet with a boy at school called Robert Evans. 'I'll never like girls,' he says. 'Well,' I reply, 'I agree that girls are yuck, but we'll both change our minds. All grown-ups are married. I bet you fifty cents that one day you will be too.' (I have the urge, all these years on, to try and collect.)

- My mother whacking me on the legs with her shoe, which had jewels on it.

- Cycling down to the creek that ran through some scrub not far from home. A hazy memory of other children and a raft and some 44-gallon drums. I remember the smooth surface of the very steep road – white concrete when most roads were tarmac.

Is this what most people's memories are like? Do we all miss the important bits – who were these kids with the raft? – while having really sharp recall of the colour of the road surface upon which we pedalled?

*

My parents might seem eccentric but at least some of their oddities were in keeping with the time. Parents in the 1960s were often quite uninvolved in their children's lives. Most didn't attend weekend sporting fixtures in the way that's common today. Back then, children would cycle to the ground, play a round of football or cricket, and then cycle home. Most primary-school children would travel solo to school and head home again at the end of the day. And the whole project of engaging with your children – praising them and cheering them on – was not even considered. Worse, the merest flicker of praise was condemned as something that might produce a child 'with tickets on himself' or 'too big for his boots'.

Five decades on, parents are criticised for being too upbeat about their children's achievements – the 'culture of unearned praise', it's now called – yet the earlier generation of parents took it to the opposite extreme. The parents of the 1960s and 1970s acted as if it would kill them to say something positive.

In most households, you'd have had variations on this discussion:

'Hey, Mum, good news – I scored 99 out of 100 in the French test.'

'Oh, what a shame. You'd better work on the word you messed up.'

'I also got 99 out of 100 for mathematics.'

'That's why you should have studied harder the night before. And don't use the word "got"; "received" is better.'

'Well, Mum – what about this? I *received* 100 out of 100 in history.'

'Don't brag, darling. It's not nice.'

It's true that optimism and modesty are fine qualities. But could it be that the parents of the first chunk of the twentieth century rather overdid things?

I imagine Einstein emerging from his bedroom: 'Mother, good news, I have just unified space and time in one theory. I'm calling it my Special Theory of Relativity.'

'Albert, Albert, don't be a show-off. No one likes a bragger. If the theory is so special, you should let other people say so.'

Or Sir Edmund Hillary, back from Everest:

'I made it, Dad.'

'Well, that's good, son, but it's no reason to tramp snow into the living room.'

*

At the beginning of 1971, when I was twelve, we moved to Canberra. Or, to be more accurate, it was decided that I should move to Canberra. My parents had purchased a newsagency in the centre of town and had to wait a few months before taking possession. It was arranged that I should be sent ahead, like a tiny emissary, so I could start at my new school. For the first part of the year, I was to live with an old newspaper friend of my father's. This fill-in father was Stanley Hutchinson, the chief Canberra correspondent for the Fairfax newspaper group. With his wife, Bette, he lived in a huge company-owned house opposite my new school.

I have sunny memories of their place: wandering in an overgrown garden that seemed more like a farm than a suburban plot. I slept in a room vacated by one of their grown-up boys and was astonished by my sudden exposure to ordinary, loving, family life. No regular nights with babysitters. No being sent upstairs to bed with the babble of a party below. No glamour-struck mother wearing designer clothes. The Hutchinsons had a dog, a labrador called Honey, who would lie at my feet, her tail languidly wagging. There was a warm kitchen and a lived-in, tatty feel to the rooms. You can see why I found it enormously strange.

I think most children have this experience at some point. It's only when they spend time in someone else's house that they realise the spectacular oddity of their own: 'Oh, I get it. This is what normal people do.' And Bette (I don't want to get maudlin here) showed real affection for me. She was very pleased to have a new, young son to replace her grown-up boys; she even, in defiance of the times, supplied the odd word of kindness and praise. And because the school was just over the road, she suggested I come home each day for lunch, at least while I was settling into my new surroundings. She'd make daily treats of tuna bake and shepherd's pie, all cooked in ancient Pyrex dishes, Bette looking at me fondly as I ate, an apron tied around her waist, a wisp of hair escaping her scarf, like an image from a pancake packet ...

Hang on, I promised not to get maudlin. What can be done? At this point, I may need a humorous tale to lighten the mood, perhaps something involving my testicles. Ah yes, that's right, it was around this time that my testicles decided to tie themselves into a knot, much in the way of the old song:

Do your balls hang low? Do they dangle to and fro?
Can you tie 'em in a knot? Can you tie 'em in a bow?
Can you throw 'em o'er your shoulder like a regimental soldier?
Do your balls hang low?

The testicle thing happened a couple of months into my stay with the Hutchinsons. We were driving out of Canberra, headed for Cooma. My fill-in parents were in the front of the car and I was in the back. Suddenly I became uncomfortable in the trouser department. Worse than uncomfortable. I felt this searing pain. I squeezed my legs together, willing myself not to say anything. While the Hutchinsons were lovely people, this was just too embarrassing.

At twelve years of age, it can be difficult to work one's testicles into the conversation. Trying not to draw attention to myself, I gingerly prodded at my pants. I squirmed in my seat, hoping the agony would pass. Weirdly, I can still remember the view from the window. I could take you back to the exact stretch of road, the pain having branded the view into my memory.

I rely on Wikipedia for a description of what was happening inside my body:

> Testicular torsion occurs when the spermatic cord (from which the testicle is suspended) twists, cutting off the testicle's blood supply, a condition called ischemia. The principal symptom is the rapid onset of testicular pain. Irreversible ischemia begins around six hours after onset and emergency diagnosis and treatment is required within this time in order to minimize necrosis and to improve the chance of salvaging the testicle.

Necrosis? Salvaging the testicle? I'm not a doctor, but that doesn't sound good. Little did I know it, but my twelve-year-old ball was hanging by a thread; a thread that had tied itself in knots.

From this distance I want to shout to my twelve-year-old self, squirming as he was in the back seat of the car, heading up the Cooma road, in a direction that led away from the nearest hospital: 'Hey, Richard: say something! Get over the embarrassment.

Necrosis could be minutes away.' But my twelve-year-old self doesn't hear. He just squeezes his legs tighter and grinds his teeth together and stares out the window, hoping this will pass.

'Irreversible ischemia begins around six hours after onset …'

Perhaps I should enlist the help of any possible future children and get them to shout out to him: 'Hey, Dad, you really should say something, otherwise your balls will die and with them any hope of us being born.'

'… diagnosis and treatment is required within this time to improve the chance of salvaging the testicle …'

Back in the car my twelve-year-old self sweats and squirms. He comes close to saying something, but his face flushes red with the thought.

Perhaps his future wife, should he ever have one, could intercede? 'Come on, Richard. The day will come when those balls, absurd though they may be in appearance, will be considered with affection by someone, perhaps even by me, so don't let them turn black just because you are here with these people you don't really know, having been abandoned by your somewhat peculiar parents.'

Ah, that seems to have done the trick. Back in the car the twelve-year-old boy overcomes his embarrassment with a sudden yelp of pain. Bette looks around in concern. Stan stops the car. They can see how the blood has drained from the boy's face. He tells them where it hurts. They turn around the car and head for Canberra Hospital. At the hospital, the doctors administer a general anaesthetic and the pain drops away as the boy counts back from 100: 99, 98, 97, 96 ...

My parents must have come down to Canberra to see me in hospital, but I don't recall their visit. I just remember the doctor as I came out of the anaesthetic. He sat on the edge of the bed and said, 'I don't know if you understand what I'm talking about, young man, but if you had been just an hour later then you might have missed out on children of your own.' I have since checked this with a specialist and his diagnosis may have been overly dramatic, as you'd still have one good ball. Still who wants to look like Hitler?

Oh, glorious chapter that has an opportunity for two testicle-related ballads:

Hitler has only got one ball,
Göring has two but very small,
Himmler is somewhat sim'lar,
But poor Goebbels has no balls at all.

*

I don't know why my parents left Sydney and bought the newsagency; in retrospect, it makes little sense. The explanation given at the time was that my father was sick of working for others and wanted his own business. Yet both my parents had good jobs and seemed to relish being part of what passed for high society in Sydney. Perhaps my father's drinking was starting to build in a way that gave him trouble at work; maybe my mother was having an affair. I have some recollection of angry words between my parents, centred on a particular man, a famous businessman. More likely, though, it was just the allure of money: a couple they knew had a newsagency in Sydney's Double Bay and had installed their 25-year-old son as the manager. He earned so much money he'd purchased a suit worth $200. That sum of money – $200 – was such an incredible amount for a suit. My parents talked about it endlessly. The newsagency business must be a goldmine to allow the purchase of such a suit. Life twists and turns on the smallest of things and, in all likelihood, it was that suit which sent me to Canberra – and thus to my particular adolescence, my particular school, my particular teachers.

And, in a way, to a right ball that, ever since, has hung rather low.

Chapter Two

After a few months my parents arrived in Canberra. I said farewell to the Hutchinsons with a stab of regret, moving my stuff from the upstairs bedroom, saying goodbye to Honey the dog, the overgrown garden and the snug kitchen. My parents rented a large house with a separate wing – consisting of two rooms and a bathroom – into which I was installed. There was even an intercom to the rest of the house, via which I could be summoned to dinner. This was fun at the time but, as I type this, does seem a rather obvious metaphor for my emotional separation from my parents. I apologise, dear reader, for constructing my childhood from such heavy-handed literary devices. In my next life, I will insist that reality expresses itself through more subtle tropes.

Sitting in my separate wing, I began to develop a passion for Elvis Presley, bordering on monomania. Looking back, it seems entirely clear that I was reaching out for some sort of father figure, and found one in the most unlikely place: inside a white jumpsuit spangled with rhinestones, satin straining around the belly. With access to a newsagency I would bring home great piles of newspapers and magazines and search out the merest mention of the King. I'd cut out the paragraph and Clag-glue the clipping into a massive scrapbook. Elvis, by this time, was past the height of his fame, so the clippings were meagre: tiny mentions of his films screening at midday on Channel 7, the scraps so small that my painstaking annotations – '*TV Week*, June 26, 1971, page 34' – took up more space than the clipping itself.

By the end of that first year at school, my report card put it bluntly: 'When the adulation of Elvis Presley diminishes (the sooner the better) and Richard's energies are channelled to more constructive ends, his overall performance will improve further.'

I'm aware you'll think this is an attempt at comic exaggeration, so I've scanned in the report so you can see for yourself:

Alas, by the start of the second year of school, my obsession with Elvis had grown even stronger. The walls of my separate wing were papered over with Elvis posters and record sleeves. I insisted on completing a school project on Elvis in which I displayed photographs and text around the headline: '1954 to 1972 – 16 great years of Rock and Roll', my skill at Letrasetting proving superior to my talent for mathematics.

*

At this point I moved into a class with a new English teacher: Mr Phillipps. In a Canberra private school in the 1970s, he was everybody's image of an old-fashioned British academic. The final two 'p's in his name seemed to pprove it. He would address each student as 'old boy' and endlessly read aloud from his collection of ancient Penguin paperbacks. In retrospect, I can see he was pretty delighted by his own sonorous voice and upper-class accent. Mr Phillipps certainly gave his voice, and his credentials, a real workout. Rather like my mother, he was a 'lavatory' man. And a 'sofa' man. And a 'spectacles' man. He had wiry dark hair and a clipped DH Lawrence-style beard, like it was copied from the photo of Lawrence on the back of the Penguin paperbacks he was reading. Summer and winter, he would wear an ancient blue jacket onto which was stitched the crest of the Oxford college he had attended decades before, teamed with fawn trousers and an Oxford tie. He would mention, quite often, that he had been personally taught by JRR Tolkien and CS Lewis. Occasionally, on a sports day, the jacket would be exchanged for a white cable-knit jumper, also bearing an Oxford logo – one which, he said, indicated he had a 'blue'. In the Australian schoolyard of the '70s a 'blue' still meant an argument, normally involving fists, but we did our best to look impressed.

He was precise in all things. He'd move slowly, deliberately, whatever the task, as if he was enjoying his own body and the elegant way it moved. I remember watching him, one day after school, approach his car. First he placed his briefcase on the bonnet. Then he opened the latch of the briefcase. Each of these was a separate movement, with a conscious and deliberate beat in between. Next he fished down into the briefcase – separate movement – located the keys and pulled them out – separate movement – set them on the bonnet – separate movement – relocked the bag – separate movement – and finally reached for the door. It's not that it took him ages to drive off, just that every stage was somehow self-regarding.

For all that, he was passionate about his subject. An example: when I was thirteen, he became concerned about my progress with Shakespeare. In the middle of Year 8, he suggested he could give me extra lessons. He offered to meet me each Saturday morning in a small office close to our classroom. I agreed. For all my difficulty understanding Shakespeare, I loved reading and I loved writing. And so our arrangement began: I would cycle from home on Saturday mornings, arrive at school at nine, and be treated to a couple of hours of free, private tuition. Canberra, in midwinter, was cold. Cycling meant a scarf wrapped around my head, a slit for my eyes, like I was wearing a hairy burka. My hands would sting as they gripped the handlebars, my eyes streaming with the cold. I was a martyr to literature. Yet I felt lucky to have been offered this doorway into a sophisticated, literary world.

Mr Phillipps was a patient teacher, encouraging me to recall and explain Shakespeare's plots. After a few weeks, we naturally moved on to a study of Samuel Pepys, the great English diarist of the seventeenth century. Pepys famously detailed the Great Fire of London as well as the bubonic plague of 1666. For a thirteen-year-old, his diary was a revelation. He wrote so vividly, the personal and the political in perpetual collision. Building on my enthusiasm, Mr Phillipps suggested I write my own diary. I loved the idea, scribbling my thoughts day by day into a small exercise book. On subsequent Saturday mornings Mr Phillipps and I would critique and analyse what I had written. Had I made the same decisions as Pepys? Was my writing as powerful as his?

It was only later, a lot later, that I realised the whole thing had been a ruse. Actually, quite a cruel one.

*

Meanwhile, in a piece of perfect timing for my parents, the Whitlam government was elected. The public service grew in size and Canberra boomed. The newsagency was raking in money. My father could have bought $200 suits every day. We moved from the rented house with the separate wing and bought a smaller but very chi-chi house on the same street as The Lodge, the official residence of the prime minister. The house had been owned by the man who ran Canberra's Lobby restaurant, a favourite haunt of politicians and journalists. It looked like a decorator had been hired to fit out both business and home. The interior design hovered in some weird 1970s combination of hippy retreat and upmarket brothel. Several of the doors featured sheets of heavy, patterned glass, covered in ruby-coloured swirls. The wallpaper was burnished to look like metal and there was white shag-pile carpet throughout. Later, when things turned nasty and bloodstains became an occasional problem, this turned out to be a poor choice of floor covering.

Despite their disregard for each other, my parents' lives were working out in a material sense. They purchased a small rural property outside Canberra, my mother happily naming the cows and playing the gentlewoman farmer on Saturday afternoons. She was both an animal lover and a cleanliness obsessive and so took to wearing white cotton gloves whenever she went near the animals. In fact, she started wearing the gloves whenever she left the house. My father began dressing like a country auctioneer, in tweed jackets and a knitted tie. He saw himself as Lord Ted – a Lancashire man who'd done well and could jovially splash around his money. The extra-wide hallway in our new house was optimistically renamed the 'Gallery' and kitted out with outback oil paintings by people like Pro Hart and Hugh Sawrey. My father insisted on buying me a made-to-measure suit for my fourteenth birthday, even though my body was changing by the month. And he began purchasing sports cars so expensive they never worked.

The main activity I shared with my father was helping him count the family cash: he'd bring home bags of coins each day from the newsagency and we'd sit together at the kitchen table, rolling them into batches so they could be presented to the bank. Despite my somewhat difficult childhood, this book is not *Angela's Ashes* and here's why: it's hard to win sympathy from a reader once you've included the phrase 'every night my hands were black from counting the family money'.

When not counting coins, I spent a lot of time away from the house – either with my friends or walking on my own in a dreamy adolescent way, hands stuffed into the pockets of my overcoat, imagining myself a tortured intellectual. While walking, I would talk to myself. I enjoyed the chance, I suppose, to converse with someone whose intellectual ability I found so impressive. I was regularly stopped and questioned by the police. It was hardly surprising: I would be walking past the embassy of some troubled country in a padded greatcoat, mumbling inanities. After a few questions, the police would realise I was merely a self-involved idiot and send me on my way.

I was bookish and effete and found a peer group of other would-be intellectuals. We were pretentious and ridiculous, of course, competing with each other as to who would be the first to claim they'd read Camus or Sartre. All I actually read, of course, was my own body weight in PG Wodehouse and Dorothy L Sayers, and yet we were the sort of boys who would give our bedrooms a makeover before the arrival of any visitor: positioning a copy of WH Auden's poems by the bedside; propping some Brecht open on the desk; and idly dropping a copy of the *New Statesman* on the middle of the floor. I still have a copy of *Thus Spake Zarathustra* inscribed by my friend Toby: my present for turning fourteen. What twats we were.

Yet perhaps Toby was prescient in his choice, as a fair measure of *Sturm und Drang* was about to enter my life.

*

David Phillipps had not only been taking me for special lessons on a Saturday morning, he'd also, a year on, established a 'drama reading club', inviting me and my peer group to come to his home and read aloud a classic play. On one occasion it was Arthur Miller's *The Crucible*; another time something by Chekhov. I don't recall how often we did this, but I do remember arriving once when Mr Phillipps' wife was walking away from the house. She was dressed in squash gear, with a racquet in her hand and a pissed-off look on her face.

It didn't occur to me to question the point of these classes. Did Mr Phillipps hold these clubs for each age group, or only for those in Year 9? If for Year 9, why was it just me and my friends who'd been invited? We were neither the very top of the class nor the bottom: 'Oh, yes, it's those ranked third to fourteenth that I particularly like to help.'

Equally with my private lessons: I used to come eleventh in English. In what strange world does a teacher suddenly recommend special private lessons for the kid who is coming eleventh? 'Those kids who come eleventh, they are the ones in whom I specialise.'

*

One night, Mr Phillipps appeared at our house for dinner, dressed in his usual Oxford jacket with crest, fawn trousers, blue shirt and Oxford tie. I don't recall the dinner – tense, presumably – I just remember the explosive moment on the front steps as Mr Phillipps was taking his leave and my father began to warn him off. 'Don't come again. I don't want you making contact with my wife.' It got heated. A raised voice from my father; pomposity from Mr Phillipps: 'I say, don't you dare raise your voice to me.' There was pushing. Mr Phillipps left and then my father shouted at my mother, grabbing her arm. I stepped between them but he kept yelling, his hand still on her. Effete boy me, I punched my father in the face. He stopped shouting and looked sad. He didn't punch me back. The whole thing defused. I went walking.

*

What followed was a period of constant disputation. It was obvious there was something going on between my mother and Mr Phillipps. My father, always an enthusiastic drinker, started hitting the stuff pretty hard and my mother rewarded him with ever larger servings of contempt. My father was never physically violent towards my mother, but he did take out his anger on the household's doors, slamming them repeatedly. Our otherwise presentable home ended up with dramatic cracks around the architrave of each doorway, as if the whole place had suddenly been shifted into an earthquake zone.

A month or two after the dinner, the argument, and my ill-considered punch, Mr Phillipps and my mother ran away together.

I'll say that again, just so you can savour my humiliation: My mother ran off with my English teacher. In term two, my mother disappeared, and so did Mr Phillipps. Presumably, he'd fallen for her at parent–teacher night, which somehow made it worse. My fellow students were so flabbergasted they couldn't bring themselves to tease me. The situation was clearly so hilarious and embarrassing and awful that even a group of rowdy Australian schoolboys thought: 'Nah, too easy.'

The day before she left, my mother came into my room to tell me of her decision. I was sitting on my bed and she stood in front of me. She and Mr Phillipps intended to go first to Sydney and then to a country town about ten hours north. She said she loved him. My mother reached out and held both my hands. She looked into my eyes. She said: 'Thank you for finding him for me.' It was as if the whole thing was my idea.

Going through my father's papers years later, I found the note she left that next day:

Dear Teddy

Have left everything as tidy as possible. Please be everything Richard wants of you. Let him be able to admire your strength, please the boy needs this. Keep your chin up + help Rich. Give Marie the gloves left on the table.

PS: As an afterthought I have taken the sherry decanter.

I'm sure, by this point, you are ahead of me in terms of Mr Phillipps and the private English lessons he'd been giving me every Saturday morning. In retrospect, it seems so terribly obvious: the way Shakespeare led to Pepys and then Pepys led to my own diary, and how Mr Phillipps would take away my diary for 'marking', examining these jottings about my life at home, my parents, my mother ...

The private lessons, of course, were a way of finding out more about my mother; a method of gaining access and knowledge. They were a trail of sugar cubes leading to a trap. What's strange is that I didn't work this out at the time. It actually took me years. I still can remember the moment decades later, idly thinking about those lessons, and the sudden flash of revelation: 'Hey, hang on a minute ...'

The lessons made me feel special at the time, but Mr Phillipps had been striding eagerly towards my mother, and I was his gangplank.

Chapter Three

My mother having left, things turned ever more chaotic. My father spent his nights sobbing with rage. He was drinking without mercy for himself or anyone else. He'd run the shop by day and then return home. Often he'd give me the same speech over dinner: 'In there, everyone thinks I'm great, everyone thinks I do a wonderful job, but as soon as I get home everyone's at me.' Actually, no one was there to be 'at him', only me, and I don't think I minded him so much. Of course, there was also a difference between the apparently much-praised 'Work Ted' and the apparently much-maligned 'Home Ted'. 'Home Ted' had, by about 6.30pm, drunk so much he could hardly stand.

I'm sure my father had really loved my mother, despite their strange, sexless marriage. He was certainly sent sprawling by her departure. Gregarious and sometimes ebullient, he also had a shaft of depression and self-pity. He'd never been the man to fulfil her lofty ambitions. For a few months after my mother's departure he staggered on, but his mood seemed to increasingly darken. Maybe he'd expected her to maintain some contact; perhaps he'd hoped that she'd visit the two of us. Instead, she vanished. In the end, my father decided to return to Britain for a break. As an attempt to shake off his misery, he booked himself a three-month trip during which he'd stay with his mother and sister.

As luck would have it, one of my father's friends was moving to Canberra and it was arranged that this old mate would look after me. The only catch was that he wouldn't arrive for a while. So here was the deal: I would live on my own for three weeks and would then be joined by a temporary parent. We'd 'batch it', as was the expression for two chaps sharing a house. Looking back, this seems a peculiar decision: why didn't my father just delay his trip until his friend was ready to move in? Still, I don't remember being troubled by it. I didn't write a diary at the time, despite my familiarity with the work of Mr Pepys, but if I had, I imagine it would have been filled with observations about potential girlfriends and the pretentious books I was pretending to read, rather than the departure of either my mother or father.

My friends, of course, were keen to make the most of a house without parents, especially one with a freezer full of food and a pool. I'd like to claim it also had a well-stocked bar, but as the child of any alcoholic knows, though many bottles come to visit, few hang around. I have a half-memory of one of my friends trying to get the sticky dregs out of one of my father's bottles of Blue Curaçao before realising he'd been bested by a professional. And so my friends would visit every night and we'd sit drinking tea, talking bullshit philosophy, awaiting the arrival of my fill-in father.

Occasionally, I admit, I became a little maudlin and would whine to my friends, hoping to drum up some sympathy: 'It's so unfair, my mother's run away and now my father's gone.'

Years later one of them remembered the scene with unnecessary accuracy: 'Yes, yes, Richard never really left home. Home left him.'

*

A few weeks on, my father's friend arrived. His name was Steve Stephens. All those years before, he'd helped my father set up the newspaper in New Guinea and they'd stayed in touch. Separate to the drama in our household, Steve had seen the financial success of my father's business and decided that he, too, would buy a newsagency in Canberra. That $200 suit had a lot to answer for.

By the time Steve knocked on the door, the fridge was empty and the pool had turned green. He fixed both problems with immediate good cheer. I realised, almost instantly, that I'd been sent a gift.

Steve Stephens was a craggy-faced Australian bloke. His hobbies were shooting and fishing. He always had a cigarette poked into his mouth and a talent for the Australian vernacular. He also wrote poetry, loved his wife and was fiercely loyal to my father. He was very masculine in a traditional way, as well as being reflective and generous. This sort of expansive masculinity turned out to be just what I needed.

By the time Steve arrived, events had conspired to make me a little confused about what it meant to be an Australian man. My father, for all his good points, didn't really embody what you could call masculine virtues. Selfless, forthright, practical, strong: none of these words really sprang to mind. And Mr Phillipps didn't measure up, either: he was pompous and vain, even aside from the way he'd made off with my mother. Outside these two men, there was the more general perception of the Australian man as some sort of unfeeling Ocker – a definition which involved attitudes to sport I didn't share, attitudes to women I didn't understand, and attitudes to alcohol which, well, I've been working on ever since.

My confusion wasn't particularly helped by my passion for Canberra Youth Theatre, in which I was now spending all my free time. There were some admirable young men there, but they shared a view of masculinity as extreme as that of the Ockers. The Youth Theatre group-think went something like

Me at fifteen: a confused mix of pretensions and patchouli oil.

this: that maleness is associated with violence, insensitivity and the oppression of women, and that the best thing is to hide any masculine attributes under a fluffy layer of hippydom. We would do plays about rape in war, and other light entertainment topics. Masculinity, according to this view, was a disease which could only be treated through the constant application of patchouli oil.

Steve Stephens was an antidote to this mess of competing stereotypes. During the couple of months my father was away, Steve did his best to make a man of me, in his own broad sense of that word. He took me trout fishing, the two of us standing freezing in a rushing creek in the snow country, neither of us catching anything, probably because I was talking all the time. (I hadn't previously found many adults willing to listen.) He taught me how to cook a trout, just in case I ever managed to hook one. You set a fire, heat a frypan with butter, then slip in the fish. If you lit a cigarette at the point you began cooking, the trout would be ready to turn when you finished the smoke. You'd then light another cigarette in order to accurately time the cooking of the other side.

He also showed me his poetry and made me read other people's verse. He talked to me about life. He pointed out sunsets. And he took me hunting.

On the day we went hunting, I lay on my stomach and pulled the trigger. On the tenth or twelfth attempt I shot a rabbit. All these years later I can see its death, the small spring upwards when the bullet hit. Steve, being Steve, said the only reason to shoot another creature was for food, so it was my responsibility to skin the rabbit for eating. In the end he volunteered to do the eating, but I remember skinning the poor tiny thing, standing in the gathering dusk and pushing my hand into the warm glove between the skin and the body. That day in the bush is sharp in my mind, with a mix of gratitude and nausea.

Steve was generous with his time. If I had to go somewhere he would offer to drive me. I'd feel guilty and decline. Sometimes he'd insist and I would thank him profusely as we drove along. He'd just shrug and flash me his lopsided smile: 'It's just turning a wheel, son.' Years later, when someone thanks me for giving them a lift, I repeat Steve's phrase: 'It's just turning a wheel,' but rarely explain the reference. For me, it's a nod across time to thank Steve for his kindness.

*

My father eventually returned from his break in Britain and took up the reins of the household. Steve moved into his own place. I missed him, although it's important to say that Ted put some effort into looking after me. He was certainly consistent when it came to dinner – with a never-ending supply of lamb chops and potatoes, a dish we'd enjoy on Monday, Tuesday, Wednesday, Thursday, Friday and Sunday nights. (On Saturday, he'd add half a grilled tomato just to mark the festive mood.) His efforts were marred only by an inability to leave alcohol in the bottom of any bottle within reach. By early evening, every evening, he'd be one gin short of a Hogarth etching.

With each week, he seemed to slip deeper into a slough of despond. His newsagency backed onto a car-park, on the other side of which was a French restaurant of the 1970s kind called Charlie's, all snails, pâté and Steak Diane. He took to lunching there every day, polishing off a bottle of red along with the Steak Diane, then retreating to his office at the back of the newsagency. At night, he'd come home at six or seven and cook dinner as he got stuck into the Scotch and soda, producing the soda with the assistance of a brushed-aluminium siphon. It was a device that was seen as sophisticated for reasons that now seem unclear, producing soda that was either entirely flat or so fizzy it would explode and drive all the Scotch out of the glass onto the floor. It was a wonder that, thus impeded, my father managed to get so much of the Scotch into himself.

After a year or two, my father met a woman – a widow of similar years to his own. They married and his new wife moved into the house. I liked her a lot. Almost from the start, the marriage didn't work. My father was still besotted with my mother and, given half a chance, would weep and rage, screaming about 'that bastard Phillipps', the word 'bastard' always appended to the 'Phillipps' as if it would be a grammatical error to have one without the other. As for me, I was having adventures and misadventures, and both were probably the product of negotiating an adolescence unencumbered by parenting. Some of the experiences were great and some quite awful. I don't need to recount them all, but to summarise: when a young person is unprotected and needy, paedophiles from miles around seem to instantly know, like they are on some sort of text alert. I remember at age sixteen, having been invited to stay at some older man's flat in Sydney, opening a cupboard door to see a swill of child pornography on the floor and thinking: 'How did I get myself into this? And how do I get myself out of it?'

On another occasion, a man convinced me and one of my school friends that he was a filmmaker. He had a script. It was set in Weimar Germany and was about the adventures of two young sailor boys. Yes, really: Weimar sailor boys. If there's one thing I can't stand about small-town paedophiles it's their lack of originality. I was keen to be a film star, but then my friend showed his father the script. My mate's dad, in a scene of some fury, descended on the project and chased the old creep away, saving me in the process. I suppose, all these years on, I should thank that father. In fact, we can all take pleasure in the non-existence of a film showing me rouged, mascara-ed and dressed as a sailor.

*

I finished school and found a job in Queensland. After my years of devotion to Canberra Youth Theatre, I passed an audition to become part of a theatre-in-education troupe touring schools in the outback. We'd often drive a hundred kilometres between schools each day, across vast plains of scrub, staying each night in a different country pub. Some audiences were made up of indigenous kids; more commonly they were the children of white cattle-farmers. On one occasion we met a Greek bloke who proudly told us, 'I'm the only bloody ethnic in 800 bloody miles.' Hardly anyone in our audiences had ever seen a play. This was highly useful, as they lacked a point of comparison by which to assess my truly awful acting.

I had long thought of myself as independent, needing neither parents nor anybody else. Here, on the broad plains of outback Queensland, I could test that resilience. We were a crew of three performers – me and Peter, both straight from school, and a slightly older guy with the unlikely name of Rock. We tolerated each other fairly well, despite some tension between Peter and Rock – mostly over Peter's enthusiasm for the complete product range of the Brut cosmetics company. Peter had Brut aftershave, Brut antiperspirant, Brut shampoo and Brut soap. If Brut had produced a toothpaste or a range of condoms he'd have been an early adopter. Every morning we'd jump into the enclosed space of the car, ready for the long trip, with Rock and I gagging against the Brut which oozed from Peter's every pore. In Bundaberg, where we shared a house on the coast for a few days, Rock finally snapped, gathering armfuls of Brut products from the bathroom and running out the front door, Peter in hot pursuit, and me following behind, worried they might physically attack each other. Along the beach they went, then up onto the grassy headland, Rock laughing maniacally, Peter yelling for him to give back the Brut, out towards the point, the sky huge, the mighty Pacific stretching to infinity – and then the moment: Rock's arms flung wide, an evil cackle … and a whole cabinet of Brut flying up and outwards, into the sea.

The next day Peter purchased a new set of Brut products. Being fresh off the shelf, they made him even more pungent than before. His revenge was sweet, yet also musky.

*

The towns were rough. Our bush adventure was halfway between *Priscilla, Queen of the Desert* and *Wake in Fright*. In many places, when we walked into the pub everything would go quiet, and every head would turn. Presumably someone had whispered the unlikely truth: 'Apparently they're from the Arts Council.' I have a sharp memory of ordering a round of drinks in a pub in some cattle town. Perhaps due to my father's example, I wasn't much of a drinker and so I loudly requested two beers for my fellow actors while, *sotto voce*, asking for 'a shandy as well'. Naturally, the bartender, encountering his first ever order for a shandy, announced it to the room: 'What did you say? You want a *shandy*?' Despite his lack of contact with the world of acting, the barman possessed the sort of vocal projection that Gielgud would have used to reach the back stalls of the London Palladium. Fifty cattlemen turned their hatted heads towards the loudly advertised outrage at the bar.

I stood there while he poured the thing, fifty cattlemen giving me a good hard look.

*

I did the outback job for about a year, achingly lonely and frankly bored. Theatre can be creative but doing the same hour-long play ten or twelve times a week became tedious, at least to me. Lines from the play were filed in my head as markers: when this line was said, we were halfway through; another line meant we were ten minutes from the end; a third meant 'nearly bloody finished'. My boredom – my inability to be lost in the plot and the character I was supposed to be inhabiting – was more proof that I'd signed up for the wrong career. Sitting miserably in my pub bedroom one night, I decided to change direction: I would work my way up on the production side of TV drama. If I worked really hard, I said to myself, I might one day rise to become a junior stage manager working on a TV soap opera. It was an ambition that reflected a somewhat limited self-esteem. And one that, in my mind, involved moving to London.

It was at this point, aged nineteen, that I rang my mother – by this time settled down with Mr Phillipps in a distant country town – and requested contact details for her parents. As described earlier, she refused and delivered her speech about how they were posh but neglectful, and really she'd rather I didn't bother. She did, however, have one point of assistance. She told me she'd write to Lionel Harris, a man for whom she'd worked in 1970 when he tried to set up a film studio in Australia. He'd even taken a photo of me aged twelve, perched in a tree, which had once enjoyed pride of place on my parents' hallway table. Harris had been an actor in the 1950s and then a relatively important TV director in the 1960s and early 1970s, making episodes of shows such as *Upstairs Downstairs* and even directing a TV play by Dennis Potter. He lived in London's Belsize Park, an upmarket suburb down the hill from Hampstead. My mother was enormously keen for me to make contact. Perhaps she saw this as a chance for her son to rejoin British society at a somewhat higher point than the one on which she'd left it, some thirty-three years before.

In her letter to Lionel she suggested that he might have me to dinner. He wrote back and insisted he would meet me at the airport. I could stay with him a day or two and then head off to see my father's relatives. I accepted the offer.

It was to prove a very poor decision.

Chapter Four

Lionel had large bug-eyes. They protruded from a round face topped by a bald head, save for some fluff coming out his ears. He looked like a malevolent koala. His body was short, round and ready to burst, as if he'd been inflated with a bicycle pump and a halt had been called just in time. He spoke dramatically, emphasising every word, even if the subject matter was a shopping list. He also turned out to have a domineering personality. He was probably in his sixties, while I was nineteen. I can't call him a paedophile since I was old enough, at least under the law, to have made a run for it. I did learn later that exactly what happened to me had happened to a whole swag of young men, all from Australia. From the time he picked me up at the airport it took me five months to escape.

Once he had you in the flat it was hard to break free. I still find it difficult to explain why. Partly it was his ability to break down the self-esteem of whichever young man had fallen into his trap:

he'd put you off applying for a job, from taking a trip away, even from travelling into town on your own. He would smile indulgently but contemptuously, implying that you would wither without his assistance. And, after a while, the prophecy became self-fulfilling. Like most young Australians, I'd intended to find a job within a few weeks of arriving: barman or theatre usher were the usual options. I had limited funds. By talking me out of applying for anything – 'That's a bad part of town', 'I think you can do better' – Lionel's work was half done. Soon, it became difficult to avoid becoming his dependent.

He would also tempt me with stories of his influence. He could get me a job as a coffee boy at ITV's Elstree Studios, the first step on my glorious journey towards being a junior floor manager on a TV soap opera. He had contacts there. 'It will take just three more weeks,' he'd say, repeating the promise after each three-week deadline had elapsed. And then he'd say, 'I'll be so lonely if you go,' looking at me with pleading bug-eyes. So perhaps he was preying on my good side, my bad side, my ambitious side, my bankrupt side, my fearful side, and doing so all at once. At this distance, I still feel embarrassed I didn't have the strength or fortitude or dignity to say: 'This is awful, I'm leaving, I refuse to be your victim.' I don't really understand why I didn't. It was my lowest moment.

Lionel was after companionship more than sex, although every few weeks he'd more or less force me into bed, as I'm sure he'd done with at least some of the young 'house guests' before me. Afterwards he would stand in his bathroom with the door open and scrub himself with pHisohex to remove any trace of what had occurred, strangely keen for me to see how he was sanitising himself, despite the fact the sex had been at his insistence. I had a bedroom at the other end of the apartment in which I would cry myself to sleep most nights, burying my head in the pillow to muffle the sound. Amid my tears I'd plot ways to leave. I'd imagine scenarios in which I'd explain that I was going to Scotland, or leaving for France, or heading off to see my aunt, but I'd always get stuck at the point of his reply, knowing that he'd somehow talk me down, humiliate me into staying.

I then began plotting how I'd leave in the middle of the night, sneaking out without a confrontation, interrupting my own train of thought with a question: 'Since you've been here so long, maybe you should wait just another couple of weeks for that job he's promised. What's another week?'

I would also – at this point in my escape fantasy – remember that the outside door was triple-deadlocked at night.

*

Lionel had a heart condition which required daily treatment in the rooms of a Harley Street specialist and so each day would follow the same course. We'd get up, eat breakfast and then be picked up at 9am by a mini-cab driver who'd take us to Lionel's medical appointment. I'd sit in the waiting room for an hour and a half while Lionel, wearing a heart monitor, rode an exercise bike. We'd then take a mini-cab home, pausing at a bakery, where Lionel would buy huge quantities of cake which he would eat in the back seat of the cab.

I did mention, didn't I, that he was obese?

We'd spend the rest of the time sitting in his flat – me trying not to breathe too heavily, or move too briskly, due to his concern for the antique glass ornaments with which the flat was bedecked. It was as close as you could get to living in a booby-trapped tomb.

Some pages back, I pointed out that my life was hardly *Angela's Ashes*, but at this point it did bear a passing resemblance to *The Collector* by John Fowles, that mesmerising portrait of a young person imprisoned by a weirdo.

After about five months of misery, Lionel's job offer finally came good. I was given a holiday fill-in position as an 'assistant stage manager' at Elstree Studios, a few hours on the train from London. I still lived at Lionel's but had the daylight hours without his poisonous presence. At the studios, I fetched coffee and operated a sort of video clapper board at the start of each take, mainly for a soap opera called *General Hospital*. The people who worked there were friendly. I was employed for three weeks, enjoyed the experience, was good at the job … and then the holidaying employees all returned to work after their summer break.

This was considered quite unusual. Most years at least one of them wouldn't come back, and I would have inherited the position. The gig as an assistant stage manager was over and hadn't led anywhere. I was back at Lionel's full-time. In terms of my TV industry dreams, I'd aimed low and missed.

Into this sad scene I must introduce an unlikely hero: my mother. She'd come on a brief trip to Britain, planning on seeing some London theatre and visiting the Royal Shakespeare Company at Stratford. Naturally, she came to visit me at Lionel's. I was thin and drawn and miserable-looking. She rapidly deduced that I'd been caught in a trap and set herself the task of helping me escape.

She moved into Lionel's, bustling about and using her high-pitched posh voice to tell Lionel he'd been 'far too kind already' and she 'absolutely insisted' that her son not take advantage of his generosity for 'a moment longer'. Lionel did his best to fight back – 'it's really no trouble at all' – but soon realised he'd met his match. Within two days of my mother's arrival, I'd booked myself into a Hampstead boarding house, spotted in a real estate agent's window, and was waving Lionel goodbye.

I marched up the hill towards my new lodgings carting a heavy backpack containing all that I owned, but with shoulders that felt like a crushing weight had just been removed. I never saw Lionel again, although I can still recall with a shudder every corner of that house.

*

My mother and I never had an open conversation about my situation and nothing was said by either of us to Lionel. I do know that once she returned home she told my father about my plight and her heroic role in my rescue. Years later, looking through my father's papers, I found a begging letter detailing the funds she'd expended on the visit and asking that he pay her back: 'You know it took me nearly two years to earn back the money it cost to go to England to help Richard …'

I had somehow become the cause of her trip.

*

Steve Stephens must have been told about the drama, presumably by my father. I don't recall my father writing to me about it, but Steve did – addressed to my new accommodation in London.

His letter was composed at a coastal caravan park, to which he'd taken himself for the weekend with, he said, the express purpose of writing to me. In the envelope were four densely filled pages typed with a muscular hand on a small machine in the old journalists' way, the 'o's and 'p's breaking through the thin paper. It was a couple of thousand words in length, starting, after a few opening sallies, with a beautifully funny appreciation of London:

> *History heaves and pukes under every paving stone. Lift one up on a Friday afternoon and, whoops, there it is, the skulls of 500 who drank the local water a year or two back, then there's the charred remains of a thousand or so who stayed behind to stare at the fire and get warm for the first time in their lives, and never lived to tell the tale. Of course, it's the worms … There are more worms in English soil per square inch than anywhere else on earth. The fat ones are all on top, and should you take up a shovel and dig down some 20 or 30 feet, why the history of the last 500 years wriggles below you. It's not till you get up to the Cromwell era that they begin to thin down a bit. Up-stream from Westminster is the best place to find them …*

He continues in this fashion for some hundreds of words, taking the time to make me laugh. Finally he comes to the subject of my time with Lionel:

> *… which, I now understand, was a bit unbearable. What puzzles me, old son, is why the hell you put up with it for so long without giving the old sod a swift kick in the balls and marching off with the toes still*

tingling. Oh, well, all things pass, Rich. Sure, it's a platitude, but the bloody trouble with platitudes is that they are always the truth, nearly. Despite the fact that I am a cunt of a correspondent, you do seem to occupy an uncommon quantity of my awareness and wondering.

Towards the end, he abruptly talks about his regard for my father. 'Your father, Richard old son, is in many ways, and most of them are those which matter, a fine man … I love him.'

'Now enough,' he finishes. 'I'm tired of this terrible typewriter. It can't type, punctuate or spell. Look after yourself, old son. I think of you a lot. And think a lot of you.'

I hope I appreciated the letter as much at the time as I do re-reading it now. All that effort, all that love, his skill with language, his attempt to amuse me. Steve was part of my life for a shorter time than Lionel was part of it – two months as against five months – but Steve, and this is the truth, had far more impact. I'd met bad in the world, and I'd met good, and good had the louder voice.

*

My life improved dramatically the moment I left Lionel's. The boarding house in which I was now ensconced was run by an ancient and hospitable woman with literary leanings. Her name was Daphne, and, according to her own account, she'd attended Cambridge back in the 1930s. Before renting out a room she'd quiz prospective tenants about their favourite authors; accommodation was refused unless you could show familiarity with at least a couple of the lesser novels of Evelyn Waugh. While this may be considered a tad discriminatory, it did mean that the house was full of well-read young men and women with tastes as 1930s Anglophiliac as my own. After months being isolated and exploited, I was offered an instant group of friends, hand-chosen by a smart, kindly great-aunt. Within a few weeks I had a spectacularly attractive American girlfriend, conveniently living in the room across the hallway, and a British best mate in the room above. And, freed from Lionel's dissuasion, I quickly scored an enjoyable, well-paid job working for a family of cockney spivs in a theatre ticket booth in town, ripping off tourists whose only crime was a desire to see a show by Andrew Lloyd Webber.

Well maybe they deserved it.

All the young residents of the house would go drinking together in a Hampstead pub, the Flask, then tumble back nightly at ten, at which point our landlady would open her living-room door and invite us all in for 'a little whicky' before bed, serving out the Scotch as she talked to us about the novels we were reading. What bliss. The only possible downside: the house had a blue plaque, proclaiming it had been home to Robert Louis Stevenson, so I'd be woken each Sunday morning by the noise of an American tour group being instructed as to the historical importance of my bedroom.

At the end of the year I returned to Australia, applied for various jobs at the bottom end of the TV business and failed to get any of them. I was making a habit of this 'aim low and miss' trajectory. In desperation, I enrolled in a university course in Canberra, thinking I could at least claim to be busy with an arts degree while making the sort of upwards leap necessary to be allowed to serve coffee to actors in television.

One of my school friends was renting a suburban house with a converted garage out the back. It still had the roller door on one end, but someone had added a tiny bathroom. I moved in. It was dank, drab and full of mould, but incredibly cheap. I attended university while continuing to apply for jobs: still mostly as an assistant in TV, but occasionally for positions writing advertising copy in commercial radio. I have kept the rejection slips – a large pile of 'good luck with your search' and 'we are not taking applicants at this time' – that together form a sort of anti-résumé. Driven by a desire to fill the void in which I found myself, I started to focus a little more on my university degree. I also began to work at the local community radio station and to write pieces for the student newspaper.

One day, noticing a poster for a student play, I wandered into the ANU Arts Centre and offered my assistance. The producer, if that's not too grand a term, was a third-year student called Debra Oswald. I'd seen her in the student refectory where she sat with a group of other formidable women. She was also in classes with some of my school friends who, of course, were now two years ahead of me. She was staging a production of Joe Orton's *What the Butler Saw* – a favourite of mine – and was busy with the set design and decoration, wearing a pair of bib-and-brace overalls in which she looked incredibly alluring. I offered to help paint her sets, which I hope doesn't sound too much like a euphemism.

*

I wonder now what would have happened if that holiday job in British TV had led to permanent employment. I speculate about that possible me who lives in Birmingham with his English wife and two English children. He dreams sometimes of Australia, but enjoys his job as director of a long-running TV drama. Does the life I have instead, the one in Australia, depend on that failure? Does it all rest on this unusual event: all six of the company's permanent stage assistants choosing to return to work after the holidays? Of course, I'm now enormously grateful for that moment of disappointment, and for my subsequent failure to land similar jobs. Success at those moments would have robbed me of everything that came later. This is what I find so interesting: in the end, the doors that close determine your path in life as much as those that open. And even things which are painful at the time – my experience with Lionel, most obviously – end up fashioning what you are.

Not long ago, I interviewed the British chef Rick Stein, whose life story hinges on a licensing infraction which forced him to close down his nightclub and bar. He was free to reopen one room, but only if the place became a restaurant. The licensing decision, which left him ashamed and shattered, led to everything good. After the radio interview with Stein, a listener rang with a similar story about fate. He was camping close to a small town. He tried to attend the local night spot but it was full. Disappointed, he and his mates drove to a different town. At this second establishment, he was refused entry because he had bare feet. Disappointed again, he tried to charm the bouncer: 'Oh, go on, mate, at least I won't wear down the floorboards.' It was a funny line. More miraculous still, the bouncer had a sense of humour. He smiled and let him in. Our bloke, almost instantly, met his future wife. Many decades of bliss followed.

So, thank God for bouncers with a sense of humour. And full discos. And licensing police who shut down your nightclub. And those six stage assistants at ITV in London who returned to work in the summer of 1978. With their help, I'd gone home to Australia, been forced into university and met Debra Oswald. Better still, I'd met her in such an appropriate spot: on the set of a sex farce.

Chapter Five

Even though I wasn't living with my father, I kept being pulled back into the chaos of his life. He was depressed and still drinking heavily. His second wife, Ivy, was tearful and exasperated. My father had seemed such a good catch – handsome, gregarious, intelligent, a successful businessman. Then, once they were married, she realised the various design faults: the obsession with my mother, the anger towards 'that bastard Phillipps', the tendency towards self-pity, the drinking. Quite understandably, Ivy would call me up, demanding my attendance at the house. Sometimes I'd make excuses for why I couldn't get there, but often I'd drive over in my car. My father would be in the hallway, ranting. Or comatose in the lounge, sleeping it off. 'Look at him,' Ivy would say. 'What am I meant to do?' I don't think she expected me to intervene. She just wanted an act of witnessing, for someone else to understand what she was going through.

Meanwhile, the painting of Debra's theatre set had resulted in us becoming friends. One night, I thought I might see if she was interested in something more intense. I invited her back to my converted garage for dinner. The people from the main house were out for the night, so I made Debra a meal using their kitchen. I concocted Fried Eggplant, using a recipe from *The Vegetarian Epicure*, one of the world's worst cookbooks.

'Oh, I love eggplant,' Debra lied, peering at the slices, sitting covered in salt on a filthy teacloth.

'Terrific,' I answered, wishing I knew how to cook.

I had an electric fry-pan at the ready, into which I was pouring an unfeasibly large amount of cooking oil.

'You don't think you're overdoing the oil?' Debra said, over the glug-glug-glug sound of me adding more.

'Oh, I don't think you can overdo it,' I replied with what I imagined was a chef-like swagger.

I slipped the slabs of eggplant into the bubbling oil and, in a somewhat pervy way, examined my guest. She was dressed in a white cotton Indian blouse and a floaty hippy skirt. I was pleased to note afresh that she possessed quite stupendous breasts.

A few minutes later, I served the eggplant, alongside a bowl of steamed broccoli into which I'd broken an egg. I don't recall where the idea for Broccoli à la Egg came from: I don't think even *The Vegetarian Epicure* would have sunk that low. I can only suppose that the sight of her large breasts, or rather the material they displaced, had left me so dizzy with desire that I decided to throw caution to the wind and introduce a last-minute scaling-up of the meal on offer.

Spare no expense! Give the lady a treat! Break an egg over the broccoli!

With the help of the congealed egg, the broccoli looked like it was streaked in mucus. The eggplant, meanwhile, sat on its plate, puddling oil like a deep-fried Wettex.

'Actually, it's not bad,' I said, having forced down a forkload of eggplant.

'No, really, it's good,' Debra said, rocking uncomfortably from side to side, maybe in the hope of assisting digestion.

After this exchange of falsehoods, I invited her to walk through the backyard and into my damp, mould-ridden garage.

'There's only one chair, I'm sorry,' I said, pointing her towards a green vinyl beanbag.

I put on some Norwegian jazz, for reasons that remain unclear, and sat on the edge of my bed, listening as she told me about her latest theatre ideas. I offered her a glass of Stone's green ginger wine, an alcoholic beverage on which I'd spent upwards of $2.76 for the bottle.

Free drink! Egg on broccoli! Beanbag on which to relax! Really, there was no end to the luxuries with which this woman was being pampered.

A little later, I attempted to join her on the aforementioned beanbag. Remarkably, she shook me off, explaining she had a boyfriend and no interest in me, 'Well, not in that way.'

In retrospect, I should have cracked a second egg over the broccoli.

*

Despite this romantic misfire, Debra enjoyed talking to me. We started spending more time together. It was a deepening friendship rather than a romance. We were peculiarly identical: her parents, like mine, were working-class people who'd scrambled up a level, even if hers were more honest about their journey. We were both fixated by theatre. We were parsimonious with funds. We were hard workers; not whingers. I liked strong women. She was one.

I also became friends with her boyfriend, a science genius called Jonathon Howard, and his best mate, the now radio presenter Philip Clark; like Debra, they were interested in their studies and in intellectual life generally. Maybe some of their passion started to rub off on me. Debra had already written a few plays and had seen them performed: at seventeen she'd had a script chosen for the National Playwrights' Conference. Later, the same script had been produced on stage in Sydney and on ABC Radio. She had a startlingly good mind. I was thrilled, and secretly a bit pleased with myself, that I was able to call such a person my friend. We even wrote a radio comedy show together. It was called *Pete and Ron Join the Communist Party*. We recorded it for 2XX, the Canberra community station, with Debra playing the main female role, Denise, while Philip and I took on the roles of Pete (me) and Ron (Philip).

Like the fried eggplant, it was terrible beyond belief. I still have a copy on reel-to-reel tape, which I would use to blackmail both Debra and Philip, were it not that I would suffer equal humiliation from its release.

One night, Debra and I were in my converted garage, working on our latest *Pete and Ron* script, when my father's long-suffering new wife called, requesting my attendance. Ivy was a highly competent woman who took homemaking very seriously: she wanted a good husband for whom she could bake and clean and with whom she could share charming, cultured evenings. From her tone, it seemed that my father, as usual, was falling somewhat short of these expectations. Debra wanted a lift back to college and so came with me in the car, her first visit to my family home. Why did I take her when I had ample experience of the scene that would greet us? Maybe, just like Ivy, I wanted someone to pay witness to the things that I had long endured.

I opened the back door to find my father on the white shag-pile carpet in the long hallway that ran the length of the house.

He was on his hands and knees, naked except for a pair of Y-front underpants. He was badly pissed and bleeding quite heavily. Ivy was in the bedroom, having shut the door on him. The door didn't have a lock, but even so my father was too drunk to open it. He'd been kneeling in front of the door, trying to turn the handle, in the process of which he'd fallen several times against the timber, battering his own face into a bleeding mash. He turned his sagging head as we entered, not really seeing us, before slowly resuming his task, swaying on his knees and falling face forward yet again into the door-frame. I resisted the urge to say: 'Debra, I'd like you to meet Dad; Dad, Debra.'

Instead I had the usual discussion with Ivy, who emerged from the bedroom, stepping past my father.

'What am I meant to do?' she said, as she always did.

'I don't know,' I said, as I always did.

Afterwards, Debra said to me: 'Are you okay? You must be very upset.'

And I said, 'No. Not upset at all,' which was pretty much the truth.

Whenever these things happened, I had a habit of stepping outside myself and looking at them from above. I'd observe my father as if I was filming a documentary or taking notes for a sociological study. 'So this is what it looks like.'

I'd probably done the same when my mother left. And – less

successfully – when watching Lionel take his pHisohex showers. Actually, I'd developed a habit of doing it all the time, during good times and bad. Even during the day-to-day, I'd be above myself, watching, rather than in the moment. 'Here you are walking down the street; here you are standing to one side at a party; here you are eating a hamburger. And here you are standing with Debra watching your father bleed over the carpet.'

I was turning myself into an observer rather than a participant. It was understandable, but also a form of emotional cowardice, a retreat from feeling.

*

At the end of my first year of study, I shifted my enrolment to the University of Sydney. My friendship with Debra had continued, but other things were tugging me north. I had a new girlfriend who'd found a job in Sydney and I still dreamed of working in TV drama. Perhaps there was more chance if I moved close to the industry's hub? I was also tired of being dragged into my father's life, his many virtues being drowned out by his chief vice. Being constantly invited to witness the worst of him was not useful to either of us.

At Sydney University, I chose courses in History and English, started writing for the student newspaper, *Honi Soit,* and directed some plays at the university drama club. As the year went on, a few things changed. The girlfriend with whom I'd moved to Sydney dumped me and my job applications led nowhere. On the upside, I started to really enjoy my studies, finally understanding that the harder you work, the more interesting the work becomes. I also began writing letters regularly to my Canberra friend Debra.

Halfway through that year, *Honi Soit*'s one-time editor Clive James visited Sydney and I ambushed him at a bookshop signing, asking if I could interview him for his old paper. He had a film crew with him, making a documentary on Australia and how it had changed since he'd left. Clive gave me an interview on the proviso that I allow him to interview me in turn, presenting me on screen as a younger version of himself. He'd assumed I was *Honi Soit*'s editor, rather than an occasional contributor, and I unblinkingly accepted the promotion. The cameras turned and Clive asked me if my generation of young Australian writers yearned for Britain in the same way his generation had. I could have told him the truth: I'd been so desperate to break into the UK that I'd recently endured five months of misery and sexual slavery just to give it a go. Instead, I breezily gave him a lesson in Australian optimism: there was no need to fly to Britain because those days were gone, Australia was no longer a cultural desert, even in the arts it was the land of opportunity.

The pretend Honi Soit *editor, practising to be a journalist.*

I believed that answer, which was a measure of how my mood was beginning to lift.

*

Two or three times a year, I'd hear from my mother. She was engrossed with Mr Phillipps and sought little from her previous life. Maybe their relationship was one of the great love stories; I'm sure that was their view of the situation. Together they created a sealed system that required no input from the outside world: a sort of human terrarium. The terrarium was located in Armidale, where they had ended up after their hurried departure from Canberra – Mr Phillipps heading straight there; my mother following after a period in Sydney, working in her old trade of arts publicity. Armidale, I imagine, was chosen for the sake of Mr Phillipps. It had a private girls' school at which he could teach and a university where he could study for a doctorate. My mother, once she arrived, created a job for herself, convincing the university to support the establishment of a regional theatre company. The company, of which she would be founder and manager, would tour country towns staging plays for a mainstream audience, while also performing in schools. Due to her deal with the university, my mother and Mr Phillipps were given an apartment on campus.

Meanwhile, they started planning their love nest – a house on the edge of town, the design of which would be inspired by the writings of JRR Tolkien. Tolkien, if you remember, was the one who'd taught Mr Phillipps at Oxford, as mentioned by Mr Phillipps at least once every thirty seconds. The house would be called Doriath. In the world of Tolkien, I later discovered, Doriath was a place which had been surrounded by a 'girdle of enchantment' – a force-field magically established by its Queen so that no one could enter without the permission of her King. I realise quite a few couples end up with a fortress relationship – the two of them against the world – but they don't always include it in the very name of their house. My mother and Mr Phillipps could have as easily named the place 'Fuck Off Outsiders'.

Occasionally I'd talk to my mother on the telephone and often she'd find a way to mention her posh upbringing, her stories becoming ever more florid. In one version her father was high up in the government; in another he was with the diplomatic service. I remember one account in which her father became a German aristocrat, which did make it odd that he was 'working for Sir Winston': no wonder Britain did so poorly in those early years of the war. Whatever the tale, sitting on the other end of the phone, I'd mumble my assent.

Despite learning the truth from my aunt a few years before, I'd chosen not to confront my mother about her working-class past. I didn't see the point: perhaps she now believed all these stories. I also saw my mother as a negative force in my life: confronting her would be inviting a connection, an emotional interaction, and this was something in which I was uninterested. I preferred holding her at arm's length. I would be dutiful, but unengaged.

*

By the middle of the year, Debra and I were driving up and down the Hume Highway to see each other. She'd broken up with her scientist boyfriend and would occasionally fall into bed with me in a way that we would both have defined as friendship rather than love. For all the talk of 'hooking up' being a contemporary invention, this sort of friendly sex was common in the early 1980s. And then, as now, it sometimes fired into love, as it finally did for us. I can still identify the moment it happened, for me anyway. Debra was standing in front of a fireplace in her friend Andrea's flat, with the light from the candles creating a halo around her hair, like she was lit from within. I experienced the sharp sensation of being pierced. Suddenly I understood the metaphor of Cupid and the arrow. More oddly still, I felt myself landing inside my own body. I wasn't hovering above, watching, in the way I'd always done – doubting, distrustful – as if I were an actor forced to play a role called 'myself'. Suddenly, here I was, inside my own body, looking out through my own eyes, looking at her.

Luckily, she had also fallen in love with me. We became a couple, despite living apart. In between Canberra–Sydney visits we would write letters of many thousands of words. I still have Debra's. They are exciting and philosophic and I can find in them hints of plays she went on to write years later.

In one she talks about meeting my father and the possibilities of writing a play about such a person:

> Thinking about your father the other night started me off. Then in the King Lear class (obviously enough) I really began to fire. It would work a lot off that 'Reason not the need' bit in Lear and about how you can't only love people and give them what they deserve or hardly anyone would get loved at all. The father character I have in mind may be so crippled, inconsistent and nasty that he deserves, on grounds of 'fairness', to be completely cut off, but that you (in this case the child) should still respond by being more than 'fair'.

Sometimes seeds take time to sprout and Debra's wrenching and beautiful play about 'deserved love', *Mr Bailey's Minder,* emerged about twenty years later.

The letters also express her battle of confidence as she prepared for life as a freelance writer:

Almost everyone I admire, wish to emulate, or be as lucky as, never had a straight-arrow career path. It's odd, though, the way I'm losing my nerve about next year. I guess it's because plans I confidently spouted in the abstract are now becoming frighteningly close and concrete. I repeat for the hundredth time, you must help me – bolster my spirits, Richard, and I'll bolster yours.

Then, after several hundred more words of typed-out anxieties and insights, she scribbled an addendum across the bottom of the letter: 'What a shitty little letter this is. Sorry. Make allowances for love, please.'

I felt privileged to be part of what was really a dialogue with herself, disguised as letters to her boyfriend.

After six months of this, Debra finished her degree and moved to Sydney to live with me and to attend film school. We had two rooms in a huge but decrepit share house in Paddington and were immensely happy. We even began talking about how – in another few years – we might have children. It was just possible that, despite my best efforts to take various wrong turns, I had stumbled on the makings of a family.

Debra had already met my father. Perhaps it was time for her to meet my mother. What could possibly go wrong?

Chapter Six

From our share house in Sydney, the drive to Armidale took about seven hours. We were to stay with my mother and Mr Phillipps at Doriath – aka 'the enchanted girdle' – their newly completed and Tolkien-inspired home built on a rural block about twenty minutes from town. I turned into the dirt drive and saw the house for the first time: modest in size but with Tolkien flourishes. There were two symmetrical gables with a baronial central door, complete with a large brass knocker featuring the head of a lion. Nestled in the driveway was my mother's car, with 'BB' numberplates, standing for Bilbo Baggins.

We knocked on the door and it was opened by Mr Phillipps. My mother performed an elaborate welcome – pressing her hands together and stomping her feet as if performing an abbreviated Maori haka. It was her method of being hospitable while avoiding physical contact, something she associated with the transmission of germs. She asked if, after such a long trip, we would care to use the lavatory. Even for my mother this was a record: ten seconds in and already one 'lavatory'. My eyes scanned the room for napkins, sofas and spectacles.

Mr Phillipps indicated a bedroom in which we should place our bags and suggested we might care to have a swim. We changed into our swimming costumes and headed out to the pool, built in a courtyard surrounded on three sides by the house. By the time we got there, my mother and Mr Phillipps were already in position: my mother in the pool, standing in the shallow end, and Mr Phillipps striding around, naked. He had a terry-towelling hat on his head and nothing else, his chest puffed out and his stomach sucked in. His body had the all-over tan of the perpetual nudist. I knew about the Tolkien obsession, but not about the nudism. It was Middle Earth meets *Health and Efficiency* magazine. Where's an enchanted girdle when you need one? Debra and I walked towards a pair of pool lounges, onto which we fixed our eyes with the intensity of pilots trying to land an aircraft.

'Lovely day,' observed Mr Phillipps.

'Yes, lovely,' I managed to answer.

'Drink, old boy? A soda? And for you, Miss Debra?'

I turned to Debra who, whatever her surprise in having become Miss Debra, agreed that a soda water would be perfect.

We reached the pool lounges and gingerly lay down. Mr Phillipps wandered off to the kitchen then returned with a tray laden with glasses, soda water and an ice bucket, standing beside Debra's chair, his groin perfectly positioned at eye level.

'Ice?' he asked Debra, his penis nodding to signal its agreement with whatever choice she might make.

'No, just soda, thank you,' Debra said, simultaneously stretching out her arm for the glass as the rest of her leaned in the opposite direction.

'A pleasure,' said Mr Phillipps, maintaining his position by her side, ready to engage in further conversation.

A few moments passed. Debra sipped from her drink. Mr Phillipps just stood there, his penis bobbing as he moved his feet on the hot concrete. It was at that point that Debra, pivoting towards my mother and hence away from the nodding penis, chose to disclose that both of us had recently taken a course in Transcendental Meditation. This was an exaggeration: we'd been to an information night and had given meditation a lacklustre try, always defeated by boredom after the third or fourth Ommmm. Right now, though, Debra had been transformed into a devotee.

'Oh, yes,' she said to my mother, 'we are supposed to meditate regularly. It's a very strict system.'

'How often do you need to meditate?' my mother asked.

'Actually,' Debra replied, 'a lot.' She stretched out the word 'lot' so it seemed to have many, many 'o's, each one a window of escape from Mr Phillipps and his bobbing penis. 'At least two sessions a day, of, oh, at least thirty minutes each, and we haven't done it at all today so we'd better get stuck in.'

At this, Debra jumped off the banana lounge, like a soldier summoned to battle. I followed. We hurried into our allocated bedroom, shut the door and lay on the bed, breathing heavily, as if we had just escaped a mauling by lions.

'Well,' I said after a while, 'you've now met both my parents.'

*

Debra and I enjoyed a lengthy session of 'meditation', which meant lying side by side, staring at the ceiling and occasionally clutching at each other in horror. Eventually we emerged to find our hosts in the kitchen. My mother was fiddling warily with something on the stove, while Mr Phillipps prepared drinks – a beer for himself and a Campari and soda for my mother. Both were clothed; more than clothed, they were now rather formally attired. My mother had gone from a bikini to an evening gown with a necklace of pearls. Mr Phillipps the nudist, had been replaced by Mr Phillipps the Oxford don. He was wearing the costume I remembered from school: fawn, sharply creased pants, lace-up leather shoes, a shirt and a Jesus College tie, topped by a dark-blue jacket with, stitched onto the pocket, the Oxford insignia he'd earned thirty years before. His close-cropped beard looked particularly tidy; black hatching on his angular face.

My mother, at this point, was still running her theatre company, based at the local university, while Mr Phillipps was teaching at a private girls' school but hoping he might secure a position as a lecturer in English, again at the university. As we walked in, my mother was describing an academic with whom she was feuding, calling him 'a common little man from a two-up, two-down in Yorkshire'. I resisted the urge to point out that this was precisely the form of accommodation from which she herself had sprung, albeit one county along. Instead, for the amusement of Debra, I invited my mother to expand on the subject of her background.

'Well,' I said, 'not everyone can have posh parents like you.'

'I suppose that's right,' said my mother. 'Still, it was hard for my parents, working in India.'

I tried not to glance towards Debra but India was new.

My mother, as she stirred something on the stove, talked about the British Raj and how people such as her father would spend years battling the Indian heat, all for the sake of Empire.

With mischievous intent, I asked for specifics of his official position. 'Was he Viceroy, Mum?' I inquired.

'Oh, nothing *that* posh,' said my mother matter-of-factly. 'He was *Deputy* Viceroy.'

I was still trying not to glance towards Debra, but I could sense her astonishment. I'd told her the stories of my mother's fake past without daring to hope they'd become quite this ridiculous. Next thing, my mother would be serving a Rajasthani curry and describing it as 'an old family recipe'.

Mr Phillipps suddenly leapt to his feet. Perhaps he knew this stuff about India was all rubbish and was trying to prevent my mother from digging herself in deeper. Maybe. Possibly. I don't really know. Anyway, it was about to hit 7pm, which meant that Mr Phillipps was scurrying towards the television set. It was time for him to indulge his great daily passion, his raison d'être, his personal obsession: catching out the ABC newsreader in grammatical errors. He turned on the set and made himself comfortable as the news theme played and the announcer began his bulletin. Mr Phillipps didn't have to wait long. 'I think, old boy, you'll find the phrase is "the motorcycle gang *was* …".' He looked up and smiled at my mother in triumph. You could tell he was thinking: 'Oh, yes, a group-noun disaster in the first item; this will prove a bumper half-hour.'

The next item passed, alas without error, but soon there was a clump of pleasurable mistakes.

'Why, oh, why can't they understand the use of the subjunctive …'

'An eccentric way to pronounce the word "kilometre", if you don't mind me saying so, old chap.'

(Hoots) 'Fewer! Not Less! Fewer!'

With each of his triumphs, Mr Phillipps would look around the room, inviting our congratulations. Each time, my mother would applaud excitedly, rapidly clapping her hands while holding them close to her chest, halfway between prayer and acclamation.

Mr Phillipps was often like this. Much of what came from his mouth was either an attempt to boost himself or to put others down. In the same way, much of his conversation was designed to show off his large vocabulary, even if – now I think back – it was the same handful of ten-dollar words that were employed to make the point:

Discombobulated.

Peripatetic.

Post-prandial.

I have nothing against these words. I sometimes use them myself. But when Mr Phillipps used those words, it was his way of saying: 'Look at me, I am special.'

This linguistic showing-off, though, was nowhere near as offensive as the way he talked about others – from the fellow teachers at his school to the local business people. Everyone was beneath him; the whole world had 'contemptibly low standards'.

Back in the TV room, Debra appeared to have a plan to dispel Mr Phillipps' cloud of negative thinking. As the TV news came to an end, she introduced the subject of the just-released French film *Entre Nous*. 'Everyone I know loved it,' she said. 'Our friends from university, my sister and my dad.'

The story was chosen for its upbeat spirit. What possible negative response could any possible person have to the story of a positively perfect film which everyone positively adored? Debra's conversational offering stopped Mr Phillipps dead, for approximately four seconds.

'Oh,' said Mr Phillipps, waiting out the four beats – one, two, three, four – 'your father speaks French, does he?'

'Well, no,' said Debra, 'he reads the subtitles.'

Again there was a pause in which Mr Phillipps considered the enormity of this admission.

'I don't know how he bears it,' he said finally. 'When one is familiar with the language, one finds subtitles to be an abomination. Whenever I'm watching a film with subtitles, I find I have to put my hand up thus …'

At this point Mr Phillipps mimed himself at the cinema, his chin cocked upwards, his mouth set in a supercilious grimace, his arm stretched out in front of his face, his hand turned horizontally to block out the lower part of the screen. He held the pose so that some of the imagined film could play out in French, his linguistic skills allowing him to comprehend each word as it floated from the screen. My mother, standing at the kitchen bench, swooned in admiration: 'Oh, yes, he's fluent in six languages.'

There was another pause, finally broken by Debra. 'I think Richard and I ... well, we do need to fit in our meditation before dinner.'

*

We returned twenty minutes later. The one inescapable appointment for both parties was dinner – held at 8pm in keeping with upper-middle-class British tradition. The dining room was formal, with a polished table, elegant chairs and a grand marble sideboard. For this first night, my mother had cooked tuna mornay – a dish that involved a can of tuna, some frozen peas and what appeared to be a large quantity of wallpaper paste. We sat around the table looking at it warily, like animals in Africa gathered at a poisoned waterhole. Even Mr Phillipps looked a little askance. He said grace, in the form he'd learned at Jesus College, but perhaps without the conviction that God had been personally involved in the preparation of this inedible stodge: 'We wretched and needy men' – this really is the wording of the Jesus grace – 'reverently give thee thanks, almighty God, heavenly Father, for the food which thou hast sanctified and bestowed for the sustenance of the body, so that we may use it thankfully.'

My mother ladled out the food and actually it wasn't too bad, the wallpaper paste so gluey it stopped anyone talking for at least five minutes. Finally, Mr Phillipps tapped his beard clean with his serviette – sorry, napkin – and sought permission to leave the table. My mother giggled coquettishly, as if to say, 'You won't guess what he's up to!' Her husband returned a moment later with two teddy bears, both sitting on their own tiny wooden chairs. These he placed on top of the marble sideboard, one at either end. Then he headed out again, returning with two more stuffed toys – a lion and a zebra. There was more coquettish giggling from my mother. This went on for some time, Mr Phillipps ferrying into the room the couple's considerable collection of stuffed toys – some of them characters from *Wind in the Willows*; others from AA Milne; still more from Narnia. There was also a small army of teddy bears. By the time he finished, we were surrounded by furry forms on all sides, the candlelight glinting in their tiny orange eyes. It was even creepier than the nudism.

I understood, as I observed their behaviour, that they saw their enthusiasm for stuffed toys as enormously endearing and charming. They viewed it, if I read them correctly, as expressive of a certain Englishness: the sort of enthusiasm that might develop between, for example, two British aristocrats unaccountably detained in a dull country town on the wrong side of the world.

My mother giggled some more. 'Well, say hello to them,' she trilled in her best Queen Mother voice. And so Debra and I rose from our chairs and worked our way around the room, addressing individual teddies as required, and shaking the occasional paw when pressed.

'Isn't this one a fine fellow?' my mother cooed, pointing to a rabbit dressed in a tartan jacket.

'Yes,' I found myself answering, 'he really is a very fine fellow.'

Then from Mr Phillipps: 'This chap is called Gombrill.' And here he would put on a deep voice, in order to speak for Gombrill – 'Hello, young Miss Debra, I'm Gombrill' – leaving Debra to sheepishly reply, 'Hello, Gombrill.'

Further discussion ensued with all the stuffed toys, including an earnest to-and-fro with some giraffes, as voiced by Mr Phillipps in a yearning alto: 'We all have rather long necks!' to which view Debra added her concurrence, addressing the giraffes directly, 'Yes, you really do.'

After some minutes of this, I touched Debra on the shoulder, guiding her away from a group of lions to whom she was, of necessity, offering compliments on the luxurious state of their manes. We scurried to our room, muttering about the need to meditate once more.

The Maharishi is a harsh taskmaster.

*

Day two saw some more pool-based nudism and some resultant bouts of meditation. By 8pm we were back in the formal dining room. Thankfully, it had been cleared of soft toys. My mother had cooked Welsh Rarebit, her optimistic name for badly burnt cheese on toast. Mr Phillipps was back in his Oxford clothes, delivering his Oxford grace: '*We wretched and needy men ...*'

I suddenly understood why he always used the Jesus College version. The wording was perfectly suited to my mother's cooking.

Mr Phillipps took a bite of the food and shook his head in delight. 'Superlative work, Hobbit,' he said, using his pet name for my mother. The phrase earned a delighted giggle. We ate as Mr Phillipps entertained us from his store of meaningless whimsy. 'I think I might go and varnish my grandmother,' he said, eyes sparkling at his own *Goon Show* zaniness, and we laughed dutifully as if Oscar Wilde himself had been present.

After a few more hilarious sallies, Mr Phillipps and Debra cleared the table, leaving me and my mother momentarily alone.

My mother returned instantly to the topic which had long been a staple of our phone conversations: 'You know, Richard, I have to thank you for finding him.'

'Sure, Mum.'

'And helping me escape your father.'

'Sure, Mum.'

'He was a terrible man, your father. Even in New Guinea, he'd get so drunk. I remember him crawling up the front path to the house, so drunk he couldn't stand.'

I didn't say anything for a second. It was all too familiar. Just how many times in the years since they'd separated had I been forced to listen to one of my parents attacking the other? It wouldn't be hard to calculate: by this point, I was ringing my mother more regularly, maybe once a month, and my father every couple of weeks. Each time I talked to either they'd get stuck into the other, so let's say twelve plus twenty-four is thirty-six per year, plus an aggregator for my dad, since there were a few years in which we were living in the same house. So, by this time, I'd heard their mutual insults on several hundred occasions, either my mother's 'Your father was a horrible drunk', or 'That bastard Phillipps' from the other side. It's amazing they didn't get on better, since they shared such an identical hobby: bad-mouthing each other to their son.

But I didn't say any of that. Instead I declared, with some aggression: 'Mum, I don't want to talk about it. I hate always having this conversation with you.'

At this point, Mr Phillipps, concerned by the sudden tone of disputation, emerged swiftly from the kitchen, a fluffy object in his hand. He held it aloft. It was Toad from *Wind in the Willows*. Mr Phillipps stood at the head of the table and waggled the toy at the two of us. He used his deepest voice: 'No one has noticed my fine new waistcoat.'

There was a pause. My mother and I were too enmeshed in our stand-off to participate, but by then Debra had also re-entered the room.

'Yes, Mr Toad,' Debra said in a flat, defeated monotone, 'it really is a beautiful waistcoat.'

The conversation, as planned, rapidly shifted to Mr Toad and his attractive attire. Mr Phillipps then moved on to the subjects of DH Lawrence, the poor standards of Australian universities and the lessons he'd learned at the feet of JRR Tolkien. He spoke on this last subject for some time. If my memory is correct, for about ten weeks.

Come the next morning we left Doriath a little after 10am, pleading a sudden work crisis at home. Our five-day visit had been cut by half. We drove up the dirt road and then out onto the highway. Behind us, the enchanted girdle closed itself tight.

Chapter Seven

Occasionally, with close friends, I would tell the story of my mother and her enchanted nudist hobbit hole. Knowing my advantage, I developed a dinner-party game called 'Who's Got the Weirdest Parents?' It was entertaining but also revealing: once played, you could never again look over the red roofs of suburbia and imagine that life beneath them was anything other than screamingly odd. The rules were simple: you'd proceed around the table and each person would recount their parent's strangest habit. The participant with the weirdest parent would win the round. Sometimes victory was mine, but surprisingly often I would lose: my mother, with her nudist husband, teddy bears and fake past, would seem rather drab compared to the tales of world-class eccentricity found in the bloodlines of my seemingly normal friends.

Hilariously, there'd often be one person in the group who'd say: 'This game seems fun, but I'll just sit out and listen. My parents are so boringly normal.' But that same person – when pressed – would falter and say, 'Well, I guess Dad was normal except for the way …' And then out would tumble a tale of such frothing oddity that it would sweep all the other stories aside.

There was, for example, the tale of a father who, despite being a medical practitioner, would watch the TV with a pillow on his head, sucking a hanky, in order to cut down the radiation. Or there was the father who, despite being unemployed for two years, left for 'work' each day in a company-style car which he'd purchased to fool his family he still had a job. And then there was the finance executive who built a laundry in his carport so he could wash his clothes after a day at work because he didn't like the idea of his wife touching his undergarments.

'Is that the sort of thing you mean?' asked the man with the underwear-sensitive father.

'Oh, yes,' those at the table replied, helpless with laughter, 'that's *exactly* what we mean.'

My only hope in lifting my success rate at Who's Got the Weirdest Parents? was if my mother's eccentricities became yet more florid. Or if my father became dysfunctional enough that I could throw him into play as a two-for-one offer.

On both scores, I proved to be well placed.

*

After university, I signed up for a cadetship at the *Sydney Morning Herald*. Debra was still writing plays, plus some television scripts – *Sweet and Sour*, *Bananas in Pyjamas*, *Police Rescue*. We bought a flat in Kings Cross and then later, when we decided to try for a child, traded up to a house in Marrickville. The baby – Daniel – duly arrived, amid much celebration.

I know the stereotype is that a troubled upbringing makes it difficult to be a good parent: 'You don't know what good parenting looks like, so you have to invent it from scratch.' I didn't find it so. I loved my new role as a father, whatever the usual problems of sleepless nights and apple-juice stains on my work clothes. I found my life shifting in a thrilling and positive direction. I don't know why I found it so fulfilling and straightforward: maybe I just copied Debra, who seemed to know exactly how to be a parent.

Years later, a friend confided that Debra had been her model for the mother she wanted to be: 'She was warm and funny, committed but not hovering, ready to feed her children's interests but not push them into things; a person her kids wanted to be around.'

So I was not the only one learning from her.

Meanwhile, my mother was content inside her hobbit hole with Mr Phillipps. The two had married and my mother changed her surname (to his) and then her first name (to Anna, thus moving on from both Bunty and the original Alice). Life was good within the enchanted girdle and she had no need for anyone else. I talked to her on the phone every few weeks, but rarely saw her. That suited me. My mother was uninterested in either the new grandchild or our new Marrickville house. That said, she did inquire why we hadn't bought in Woollahra, a suburb which, during her time in Sydney, was considered the best. I explained that Woollahra was still considered the best and therefore cost many times what we could possibly afford. 'That's a shame, darling,' she said in a tone of voice which suggested, 'Well, if only you'd worked that little bit harder …'

While my father visited a few times in that first year of our baby's life, I can only remember one visit from my mother. She came when Dan was about six months old, and soon after arriving became distracted by our kitchen, which she believed was in urgent need of cleaning. She stayed about two hours and never went near the baby, instead busying herself pumping so much Spray n'Wipe into the stove-top that it stopped working for the next month. I know many people have a parent with a germ fetish but I don't think many can claim a mother who has cleaned one of their appliances to death. I made a mental note to include her compulsive cleaning and compulsive baby-avoidance in my next round of 'Who's Got the Weirdest Parents?'.

My main focus, you'll notice, still involved turning my mother into a reliable dinner-party anecdote, although I do think something started to shift in my attitude once I had my own child. I loved him so fiercely. I would do anything for him. I would never let him down. It was slightly unnerving contemplating how I'd failed to inspire the same feelings in my own parents.

I've discussed this moment with friends who had indifferent or downright rotten parents. Some have even admitted an urge to blame themselves for the fact that they were never properly loved. In bad moments, they would ask themselves: 'Was there something about me that was difficult to love? Maybe I did something as a baby or a young child to repel the love they wanted to give me.'

The idea of a bad parent seems so wrong, so against the expected rules of the universe, that we can't face the unfairness of it. We search for an alternative explanation, even if that involves cutting our own personality to pieces as we try to place the blame anywhere but where it belongs.

There must have been some self-confidence in my make-up because I never truly fell into this way of thinking. Mostly I thought myself a victim of bad luck. And if struck by a bout of 'poor-me', I'd cheer myself up by remembering a cartoon by Patrick Cook, one I'd torn from the *National Times* years before and kept inside my notebook.

In the sketch, a group of parents are looking through the window of a maternity ward. They are viewing a line of new babies, who lie swaddled in their cribs.

Says one baby to another: 'I take it there's a choice.'

That, for so many of us, seemed to sum up the situation. What happened was no fault of ours. We did nothing wrong. Through some error or oversight, we just didn't get the family we'd ordered.

*

By this time, I'd risen through the ranks at the *Sydney Morning Herald* and was in the middle of a harried eighteen months as the paper's News Editor, a job that involved working from nine in the morning until nine at night. It was an era when reporters would scream at the News Editor and the News Editor was required to scream back. One bloke was so angry about the story I'd assigned him, he picked up a metal office chair and smashed it so hard on the floor in front of me that two of the legs sheared off. He then, rather meekly, pulled out his wallet and offered to pay for the damage.

As a reward for surviving this battlefield of bleeding egos, I was handed a stint as European Correspondent, stationed in London. There was a house that came with the job and an office in a lane off Fleet Street. It was 1988 – the dying years of Thatcherism. The last time I'd been to the UK was when I was ensnared by Lionel, a period which also happened to coincide with the death throes of a government: in that case, the Callaghan Labour government of power blackouts, inflation and strikes. I specialised, it seemed, in the dying days of dyspeptic regimes. England was glorious, but only during the periods in which I chose not to visit.

As we settled into our new house, I remembered what I'd enjoyed from my first stay in England – the newspapers, the museums, the wit and intelligence so widely on display – and yet I also saw the British class system at work. The middle class and the working class spoke of each other with derision, treating each other like different species. The non-poshies would describe people who'd been to a school such as Eton with contempt, regarding them as undeserving winners of life's lottery. The poshies would joke about having less posh friends to dinner: 'Better watch out they don't steal the silver.' On radio and TV, southerners would make jokes about northerners. On one occasion Liverpool was named European City of Culture: this, according to one comedian, meant that when they stole the wheels off your car, they'd jack the thing up on a box of books. Funny, certainly, but still …

Of course, a lot of this has changed in the years since; Britain now is more relaxed about class, and generally more ebullient about life. It's a happier place than it was in the late 1980s. But, back then, there were plenty of things about the English that made me feel uncomfortable.

I noticed the way class seemed to permeate everything: two classes on my train to work; two classes for the mail; the BBC even had two TV stations – BBC1, for the workers, with shows like *'Allo 'Allo!* and *EastEnders*; BBC2, for the poshies, with a history of the Etruscan vase. Sometimes, trying to choose something to watch, Debra and I would find BBC1 too lowbrow for our taste, while the other was too highbrow. And then, of course, there were the accents – so differentiated, so precise, that people seemed to know your town, your class, and maybe even your school within a few seconds. Try picking the origins of the Australian billionaire James Packer based on the way he speaks: you'd have no idea that he represents four generations of money and power. If he were English, you'd be able to place him perfectly, probably down to the left or right dormitory at Eton.

I disliked, too, the way the poshies littered the language with words pronounced in ways wildly different to their spelling. With a slight surge of shame, I remember telephoning a professor at Magdalene College for a science story I was writing. All went well until, as part of checking his job title, I mentioned the college's name.

'It's pronounced "Maudlyn",' the professor said after a withering moment of silence. For the rest of the interview he was rather frigid, treating me as a person of no standing; an ignoramus out of my depth.

Everyone knows that 'Magdalene' is 'Maudlyn' – that was his implication – but how was I supposed to know? How was anyone supposed to know? Presumably by growing up around people who themselves went to 'Maudlyn' – sidelining not only the hapless foreign correspondent but also the vast bulk of the British population.

To me, it seemed like a way of policing social class. Don't get too uppity or you'll fall into one of our traps. You'll be invited to a house party in Berkeley Square and then ruin everything by not pronouncing it 'Barkli'. You'll be invited to dinner with the Cholmondeleys, without realising that, for no good reason, it's pronounced 'Chumley'.

True etiquette, and true class, I've always thought, is the opposite of this. Good manners are about making people feel more comfortable, not less comfortable. They're about holding the ladder up against the castle wall, and helping someone over, rather than pushing it away.

*

Australia is hardly the classless society it sometimes claims to be, yet there's not quite the same sense of people being born into a role in life – high or low – then sticking to it. Fascinated by the differences between Australia and Britain, I wrote quite often about the highs and lows of social class. Sometimes I'd determinedly pick someone from the aristocracy to interview, just for a chance to see where they lived. I loved the way their carpet was often threadbare and that – despite living in some huge mansion – their kitchen would be full of the second-cheapest brand in every category.

In one of my newspaper pieces I called it the 'threadbare carpet index' – claiming I could accurately plot someone's aristocratic pedigree from the degree of wear and tear on the hall runner: the more tragic the carpet, the longer the aristocratic lineage. Sometimes, I'd note with glee, they sported leather patches on the elbows of their jackets, regarding life as a daily choice between new clothes and the plumbing in the west wing.

To investigate the other end of the class divide, I took Debra and eighteen-month-old Daniel to a Butlin's seaside camp – the traditional working-class holiday before cheap airfares lured the crowds to Spain.

We drove south through drizzling rain to the town of Bognor Regis and found a spot in the largest car-park I'd ever seen. We carried our bags towards the entrance, young Daniel riding high on my shoulders in a backpack. Ahead was a series of grim accommodation blocks, surrounded by high security fencing. It was hard to tell whether the fence was to stop the locals from entering, or to prevent the guests from leaving.

I thought to myself, *It looks like a prisoner-of-war camp.*

Debra, walking beside me, said, 'It looks like a prisoner-of-war camp.'

As we carried our bags through the gate, I tried to reassure her. 'Don't prejudge it. Lots of ordinary British people come here. Thousands of them. They wouldn't come if it wasn't good. Trust me, this is going to be fun.'

We emerged into a central square in which hundreds of people stood in queues, open to the elements. It was unfair of us to compare it to a prisoner-of-war camp. Prisoner-of-war camps, however brutal, tend to be efficiently run. This was more like a refugee centre which had sprung up in the day or two after a natural disaster. Each family group was surrounded by a moat of kids and bags. Light rain was falling. We joined one of the queues, waiting like everyone else to be allocated a room.

Debra said, 'I can't believe these queues. This is going to take two hours.'

Again, I counselled calm. 'These guys have been running holiday camps since the 1930s. I'm sure they have a system. I'm sure it won't take two hours.'

It took two hours.

'What's weird,' said Debra, after we had finally collected our key, 'is that no one is complaining. They seem a bit miserable but not actually upset or indignant.'

This time around I didn't remonstrate. Again, I'd already had the same thought. The way this business treated its customers like scum was baffling. So, too, the way these customers accepted the shoddy treatment, with an 'It's all we deserve' shrug of acceptance.

We walked towards our room, past several large dining areas, which pumped out a smell of cabbage and stale fat. As part of booking in, we'd been allocated a meal time for breakfast, lunch and dinner – in each case, a fifteen-minute slot in which we could arrive and partake of all that was on offer. Suddenly the two hours of queuing didn't seem so bad: with its assistance, we'd missed lunch.

We dropped our bags in the tiny, bleak room we'd been allocated. I lifted Daniel from my shoulders and the three of us began a tour of the camp.

As we set off, I wondered if this was the time to sing the praises of Butlin's famous knobbly knee competitions or the even more famous Redcoats who would wander around, making jokes and chivvying everyone along.

Maybe not. The camp was tatty, dirty and broken down. There was nary a Redcoat in sight.

We reached the end of our walk and came across an 'Entertainment Precinct' that boasted a headline act: 'The Butlin's Zoo Train Ride'.

'This might be fun,' I said, with the eagerness of a person who knows he's pushed his partner into a vast vat of shit, but has just located something that might serve as a rope.

'Let's give it a go,' said Debra, with the optimism of a person drowning in shit who is keen to hear news of a rope, any rope, however questionable its utility.

The 'Butlin's Zoo Train Ride' turned out to be a mini-train which looped through a field of grass. Beside the train tracks, fibreglass animals had been installed.

I know what you are thinking: 'What's wrong with that?'; 'It sounds quite jolly'; 'How perfect for your son, eighteen months old, didn't you say?'

But here's the thing: the grass was uncut and the animals were not specially made for this purpose. They'd been purchased by some person – I assume he went by the title Camp Commandant – at an auction house for second-hand fibreglass animals. There were several large chickens, of the sort you might see outside a takeaway shop, some with slogans still affixed: 'Chicken and Chips', 'Open til Late'. Mixed in were several small fibreglass horses, wrenched from one of those coin-in-the-slot rides you'd see outside a supermarket, still suffering a pole through the head. And an elephant, souvenired from a car-wash, the trunk carrying the promise: 'Jumbo's – the Best Wash in Town'.

Other parents and children sat with us in the train, happy enough. No one seemed to think that it was all, as a poshie might say, 'a bit second eleven'.

After our seven-minute trip on the world's most pathetic mini-train, through the world's most pathetic zoo, we returned to our, um, cell. We were fractious with each other, and with Dan, for about an hour, then decided to forfeit our deposit and drive back to London.

If only we'd stayed, who knows what victories we could have achieved in the knobbly knee competition?

*

During our year in England, it never occurred to me to try to chase down my mother's abandoned relatives. That may seem odd, but I hope it represented a healthy impulse: a desire to focus on my own happy family and leave my mother's troubled past alone.

It would be wrong, though, to say I didn't think about her. Courtesy of my experiences, I started to comprehend why she had wanted to escape. Even a whole lifetime of lies might be worth it, if you could just avoid that zoo ride at Butlin's.

Chapter Eight

Debra, Dan and I headed back to Australia and our old life in Marrickville: me working as a feature writer at the *Sydney Morning Herald*; Debra writing plays and TV shows. I began to feature Debra in my column, giving her a role as Jocasta, a straight-talking, sexy, intelligent Australian woman.

In other words, a role as herself.

I'd long before become tired of the way Australians depicted themselves: the men as boofhead Ockers, unable to show emotion; the women as long-suffering doormats. These stereotypes were unlike any Australians I knew. The men I knew were emotional, loyal, family focused and would cry at the drop of a hat. The women were strong, bordering on stroppy. Okay, stroppy may be overstating it. They were, however, great mothers, great partners, hilarious after two drinks, sexy as anything, smart as paint, and always keen to do their men the favour of refusing to take any crap. The character of Jocasta was an attempt to capture all of that.

The real Debra was kinder and more forgiving than the newspaper version, but most of Jocasta's best lines in my *Herald* column were transcribed from life. I was Boswell to her Johnson. There was great pleasure in living with Debra – scribbling down her jokes – and it was a thrill being father to Dan.

The column gave me a chance to record the day-to-day detritus of life in a way that some colleagues thought a bit odd. Given a spot in the paper, why would you write about something so 'lightweight'? Why not write about politics or world affairs? I had no answer for them at the time; I just had this impulse to record an ordinary family and how it worked. Whatever the advice to the contrary, it was an urge that was impossible to put aside. Psychoanalysing yourself is always a tricky task, but perhaps it's obvious that, having been denied a humdrum ordinary childhood, I understood that such a thing was worth celebrating and recording.

Often I kept my Jocasta notebook out when Daniel was burbling away, certain I'd never be able to remember the startling logic of the three-year-old mind:

Daniel: (points to a large poster featuring a dog) What's that
   dog?
Me: It's on a poster – to sell paint.
Daniel: What paint?

Me: The paint that's on the poster.

Daniel: What poster?

Me: The poster back there – the one with the dog.

Daniel: What dog?

Or another, when we were on a bus, looking at a store with a broken window:

Daniel: Who did that?

Me: Some naughty person.

Daniel: Which naughty person?

Me: Some naughty person we don't know.

Daniel: It was Emma! It was Emma!

Me: No, someone else did it.

Daniel: Did what?

Me: Broke the window.

Daniel: What window?

Me: The one in the shop.

Daniel: What shop?

Or while watching a Robin Hood video:

Daniel: Who's that man there?

Me: It's Robin Hood.

Daniel: But it's a lady.

Me: Well, it's a lady there now. But it was Robin Hood just a second ago.

Daniel: Where's he gone?

Me: He hasn't gone anywhere. He's right there. You just can't see him at the moment.

Daniel: Why can't I see him?

Me: Because the camera isn't pointing at him, that's why.

Daniel: Where's the camera?

Me: Well, you can't see that either.

Daniel: But I want to see the camera.

Me: Well, you can't. But he'll be back soon.

Daniel: Who will be?

Me: Robin Hood.

Daniel: Where's he gone?

Sometimes, as I scribbled, I'd wonder whether my own parents would have taken pleasure in these tiny, banal moments of a young child's life. Probably not. But I had.

*

When Daniel was four, we had a second child, Joe. When he was still tiny – a week or two old – my mother happened to be in

Sydney for a meeting connected with her theatre company. She visited for morning tea, perching warily on our couch. I tried to act as if our family was normal; that my mother was normal.

I said, 'Would you like to hold the baby, Mum?'

She shook her head. 'No, I couldn't. I wouldn't know how to.'

I tried to be upbeat and peachy keen, using that jolly-hockey-sticks tone often used by people trying to make-believe they are part of a normal family.

'Go on!' I said brightly. I leant forward, the baby in my arms, offering tiny Joe to my mother, my face creased in what I hoped was an encouraging smile. I was on the balls of my feet, the baby, held in my outstretched arms, getting a little heavy as I awaited her response.

'Come on, Mum,' I said after a moment or two, 'you must have held me when I was a baby.'

'I never did,' she answered immediately. 'The natives did it.' She then shook her head furiously, as if I'd accused her of something improper.

I felt a moment of genuine hurt, of the kind I'd mostly protected myself against receiving. It felt like I'd just been slapped in the face.

I also didn't know how to interpret what she'd said. My mother was either a woman who really never had held her own baby, however unlikely that sounds, or, weirder still, she was a person who wanted to be seen as someone who'd never held her own baby.

Maybe it was simply her way of escaping the invitation to hold baby Joe – a child she assumed would be covered in germs.

It was hard to know which of the three options was the saddest.

*

My mother, by the way, may have been right about the 'natives'. My father was a keen photographer so there are plenty of shots of me as a baby and toddler. There are a couple of photos in which my mother *is* holding me, but in the vast majority I'm being cradled by the Papuan woman who lived with us, Danota.

In these photos Danota gazes at me with a look of intense love. She has beautiful crinkled black hair, worn in a sort of beehive, and a glorious smile. Her husband, Gogo, is often in the photographs too: handsome, always bare-chested, beaming at the camera. The three of us create the shape of a traditional family photograph: two Papuans and what appears to be their adopted white child.

My parents used to tell a story about having a dog in Port Moresby called Mischa that bit me so badly it had to be put down. It had its jaws around my one-year-old head and was about to despatch me when someone intervened. My mother always told me Mischa was a great dog; she assumed the attack had been caused by jealousy over my arrival in the family. But why had the dog waited until I was one year old? Danota, my mother explained, rarely placed me on the ground, instead carrying me everywhere, as was the local custom. The dog had acted when given his first opportunity; he'd just had to wait a year to have me free of Danota's perpetual embrace.

The best bits of family stories are like this: fragments which fall out when someone is busy unwrapping what they see as the main gift. I don't care about whether I was bitten by a dog. The important part of the story is the detail that's meant to be incidental: that I was always carried, that Danota treated me – tenderly, traditionally – as if I was her own. And did so for the first three-and-a-bit years of my life.

There's another set of photos, taken when I was eleven and accompanied my father on a business trip back to New Guinea. He was still on the board of the *South Pacific Post* and was required for a meeting. In the photos, we are back at our old house, posed in front of the same water tank as in some of the older shots. Danota and Gogo smile again for the camera. By now they have three children of their own, who sit grinning on the back steps. I sit among them, smiling just as vigorously. While I can't remember the words that were spoken, I remember the reunion and the fondness with which Danota greeted me.

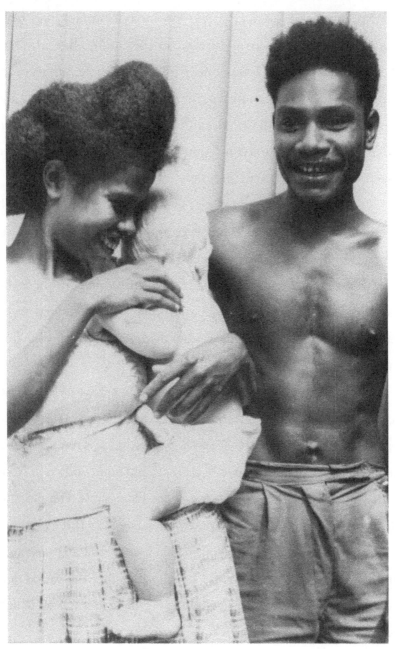

The perpetual embrace ... Danota, Gogo and me, their 'baby'.

All these years on, I know nothing about her save for these various photos. I've put Danota's and Gogo's names into Google, but there's nothing. I've written to various people who know about Papua New Guinea – 'Is this a common name? Is there some way of finding her?' – with no result. She is from a different world; I have no surname. I don't know how to summon up a trace of her, even though it may be she who gave me everything. I feel a rush of gratitude but have no way to express it.

*

While my mother crawled deeper into her hobbit hole, my father was stumbling along a course that involved many wives, many boats and many houses. There's a saying about owning boats: they only make you happy twice – first, on the day you acquire them and, second, on the day you get rid of them. In my father's case that was also true of the wives and the houses.

Every few years, Ted made some new acquisition – wife, house, boat – believing it would solve his problems. It never worked. My father never overcame the departure of my mother. And he couldn't free himself from the heavy drinking which was both cause and effect of my mother's vanishing act. Wife Two, Ivy, eventually left, her vast patience exhausted. Ted then had a year or two with a slightly younger woman, June, with whom he eventually fell out. June, like

Ivy, would ring me often, as if I was the keeper of the official ledger of my father's crimes. As my father was passed from woman to woman, it seemed they were handed the warranty booklet: 'If product fails, ring the son.'

Soon after the break-up with June, my father married Wife Three, Alice, and to celebrate he moved to Bowral, a town an hour or so from Sydney, and bought a boat for $100,000. Both the marriage and the boat started sinking almost immediately. It turned out to have rust in its innards – the boat, not the marriage – still, within a short while, he was rid of both. He then embarked on a P&O cruise – keen, I'm guessing, to find another partner, and to experience a vessel that could achieve actual flotation. On the cruise he met Robyn, a kind woman whose father was a famous stage hypnotist. She moved into Ted's house in Bowral, but seemed to lack her father's hypnotic ability to bend others to her will. My father kept drinking and – freshly optimistic about life – bought another boat.

It proved as unseaworthy as the last, developing mechanical problems that made it difficult to manoeuvre away from the marina. This suited Ted fine. He would drive up to Sydney to spend 'a weekend on the boat', which was code for two days of drinking while tied up at the dock. He had created his own floating gin palace.

It had been clear for a long time that Ted was a mirror opposite of Mr Phillipps. My mother, in her contempt for my father, had found herself a sort of anti-Ted, a human antonym. Mr Phillipps was fit, precise, disciplined, arrogant and condescending towards others. My father was loose, overweight, gregarious, generous and open-minded. Lest my comparison seem unfair to Mr Phillipps, my father was also self-pitying, depressive, undisciplined and incredibly thirsty.

Ted, more to the point, was a complainer, right in line with the northern English stereotype best expressed by Monty Python: 'We had it tough. We used to have to get up out of the shoebox at midnight and lick the road clean with our tongues.'

I'm pretty sure my father had never heard the Python sketch about the complaining Yorkshiremen. This added to my glee when, using the same northern accent, Ted described his experiences in New Guinea, speaking intently and drunkenly to me and my friend Philip.

Ted: When I was in New Guinea, I worked twenty-four hours
    a day for four years.
Me: Gee, you must have been tired, Dad.
Ted: I was. I was buggered.

It was hard to disagree. After working twenty-four hours a day for four years you would be a little tired.

Soon enough, the phone calls began from Ted's new partner, Robyn. Robyn was pleasingly tough and proud. She would ring often, complaining about my father's latest outrage. He was never violent; it was always drunkenness combined with self-pity and a belief that everyone was 'crucifying me'. As with his other wives, I was required to fill the role of witness to my father's disintegration. As usual, I felt this was unfair to both me and my father, although I understood the frustration and rage of the wives. My father was so charming when sober and so boring and unpleasant when drunk that there was a belief in each of the women that 'No one else understands what I'm going through.'

After a few months things came to a head. Exasperated by my father's drinking, Robyn removed herself from Ted's life, at least temporarily. Christmas was approaching, so we invited my father to come and stay with us for a few days. We'd sold our house in Marrickville and were renting a house in Haberfield, an inner-western Sydney suburb notable for its Federation-era homes. The whole place had been built in the early 1900s – a housing estate designed to appeal to people fleeing the cramped and dirty inner-city. Its sales pitch in 1906 was 'No Pubs. No Slums. No Lanes.' A century on, it still had most of the original houses and, by council decree, a policy of not permitting hotels. This is a rarity in Australia: unlike America, we rarely have 'dry counties'. A person can walk out their front door, and – without any local knowledge – rely on finding a pub with a brisk hike in any direction.

Cruelly, perhaps, we stripped the house of all alcohol before my father's arrival and so, on the second day of his visit, quite early in the morning, he announced he was going for a walk, which I knew was code for 'I need a drink and I can't find one in this bloody house'. I failed to intervene and explain the local ordinance, leaving Ted to head up towards the shops, his tastebuds tingling, a beer hanging enticingly before his mind's eye, the whisky chaser queued up behind it.

I'm sure he gazed from one busy corner to the next, seeing the TAB, the fruit shop, the supermarket, all the while thinking to himself, 'Surely there's a pub on the next block, there's always a pub on the next block, and if not there, maybe if I head down more towards the water …' My poor father, who probably hadn't walked more than two hundred metres at a go in the previous decade, came back two hours later, sun-struck, exhausted and still dry.

It's a sad story, I realise; one that makes two people look bad: the drunken father and his mean-hearted son.

*

Robyn constantly ended her relationship with my father, but always relented, allowing him back into her life. Sometimes she even accepted an invitation to stay on the boat. One Saturday night the boat was tethered at the marina while my father got busy tethering himself to a bottle of gin. By about 9pm he was well gone, standing unsteadily on the small deck, admiring the night sky. Alas, he stumbled and fell. Robyn, sitting inside the cabin, looked up to see my father disappearing from view. She raced up to the deck, peering into the space between the boat and the wharf, her eyes trying to adjust to the gloom. Out of the darkness came my father's Lancastrian cadences, quite cheery. 'I think I've had a tumble.'

Staring into the gloom, Robyn could just make out my father. He'd fallen onto the tangle of ropes that connected the boat to the wharf. He was suspended face-down, and yet unperturbed by his predicament.

'I just need to somehow turn around,' he said, wriggling in his cat's cradle of rope.

He had the confidence of the truly pissed, yet every time he tried to shift one way or another, the delicate hammock would begin to part, preparing to dump him in the water. Robyn – according to her own account – leaned in, trying to help, one hand hanging onto his ankle, her other hanging onto the boat as she tried to pull him closer. She soon realised the likely outcome was they'd both end up in the water. So she went to get help, bringing back a squad of passing yachties.

She stood aside, humiliated, as they hauled my pissed, ebullient father to safety.

*

Soon after the incident on the boat, Robyn began to take photographs of my father so that she could prove to me how appalling he was. There'd be a knock on our door and she'd be standing there with twenty-four freshly developed snaps, all showing my father asleep on the nature strip or passed out on the bathroom floor, head cricked up against the toilet.

'There, you see,' she'd say, fanning them out on the kitchen table, twenty-four shots of a drunken man asleep. 'What am I meant to do?' she'd ask, using the same words as Ivy, Wife Number Two, all those years before.

As usual, I had no answer, although I often wondered what the shop assistants in the rapid-print outlet thought about Robyn: these constant visits from a highly stressed lady whose hobby seemed to involve taking near-identical pictures of the same comatose middle-aged man in front of the same toilet. Call it an art project and she could have won an award.

On one occasion, Robyn went one better and took a tape-recording of one of my father's rants, which she combined with the usual roll of photographs. She turned up on our doorstep with both. It was like a *son et lumière* display under the title 'A Father's Disgrace'. Robyn insisted on pressing PLAY as Debra and I stood in the doorway. The tinny speakers of her tape-player broadcast my father's familiar complaints to the world. 'Everyone hates me.' 'That bastard Phillipps.' 'Everyone is out to *crucify* me.'

'I don't need to hear this,' I said, waving my hand to signal that she should turn it off.

'Who else can I play it to?' she asked.

In my head, I answered her: *I don't know, but not me. I've already heard this speech. I've heard it more times than you. I've been hearing it since I was fifteen. You are not proving anything I don't already know.*

All I said out loud was the last bit: 'Robbie, you are not proving anything I don't already know.'

She paused and thought about this, the tape still playing. My father, through the fuzz of the speakers, was still ranting.

'Just listen to another minute,' Robyn said. 'I want you to hear this next bit.'

We heard the next bit. And the bit after that. And then the bit after that bit. It seemed decent to bear witness to her pain.

Chapter Nine

Up in Armidale, my mother was coming to the end of what had become an impressive career. The theatre troupe she'd founded – the New England Theatre Company – had lasted twenty years, presenting a handful of plays each year to people in country towns like Tamworth, Armidale and Glen Innes. She was general manager of the company, choosing plays and directors, scrounging grants from governments, often selling the tickets herself in the box office of a town hall or school of arts, wearing her white cotton gloves to fend off the germs. She charmed local mayors, conned bargains from everyone and, despite her tiny body, helped carry the sets.

Mr Phillipps was by now a lecturer at the university. He'd completed a thesis in which he measured the stress levels of primary school principals. It was a long way from his passion for English literature, but was sufficient to earn him a PhD and a job in a discipline called Educational Administration. He chose to affix the term 'Doctor' to his name in all possible contexts.

The couple planned a retirement in Noosa, the fanciest address in Queensland, a place nicknamed 'Toorak-on-Sea' after the upmarket Melbourne suburb. They'd bought a block of land with views of the river and were having plans drawn up. Maybe, after all her years of hard work and self-denial – in both meanings of the word – my mother had achieved the bliss she'd dreamed of at fourteen: a house with a posh address, a husband with a PhD, a career mixing with the artistic elite. She'd come a long way from working-class Lancashire.

It was then – with the house planned but not built – that Mr Phillipps was diagnosed with a brain tumour.

My mother rang in tears. Her husband had suddenly begun slurring. He'd had some tests done in Armidale and the results were not good. They were coming straight to Sydney for more tests. She didn't stay with us, but I remember her at the hospital, overcome with grief. Her plans undone: the love of her life, finally secured after such travail, being ripped from her; the fortress breached.

From the start the doctors were grim. No wonder it felt unfair: Mr Phillipps had always been super-fit. He drank moderately, ate cautiously and exercised each day. My mother took him back to Armidale and put him to bed. I must have gone up to see them, as I remember him lying unconscious on a mattress, still dapper, the beard trimmed. Two weeks later he died. He was sixty-six and they'd had twenty years together.

I travelled back to Armidale for the service. My last sight of Mr Phillipps was in the funeral home: it was an open casket for reasons I didn't understand, but probably, as with all these things, connected with my mother's social class, either real or imagined. Was it a Lancastrian working-class thing? Or a supposedly posh thing? I made a mental note to ask someone, sometime, but I never have.

He was, of course, dressed in the blue Oxford jacket, with the crest of his college, Jesus. I stood alone in the funeral home chapel, looking down on him, thinking of all that had happened since that night he'd come to dinner and I'd punched my father. He had made my mother happy, I had to give him that.

The funeral was large, held in the cathedral, his fellow academics wearing their robes. The daughter from the first of his three marriages came out from England. The day after the funeral, she and I – on instructions from my mother – went through his office and cleared out anything that wasn't worth keeping. Amid the detritus, there were signs of his academic promise, of the career that had never been fully realised. He really did have a first in literature from Oxford: here in my hand was the certificate. He'd been to Sandhurst, hence the military bearing. There were radio plays, written and produced when he'd first arrived in Australia, and countless study notes published in *The Australian*, designed to help senior school students who were tackling Shakespeare or

Arthur Miller or Lawrence. As we went through them – saving a single copy, throwing out the duplicates – it was hard not to notice that they were well written and vigorous in their ideas. Maybe there was a reason for him to feel a little discombobulated about where he'd ended up: a minor department in a regional university on the wrong side of the world.

I had to admit he'd taught me things, such as how to use the word 'discombobulate' – something I'm still not averse to doing, as you can see from that last paragraph. Even 'peripatetic' and 'post-prandial' – those other favourites of his – have been known to fall from my lips. And Samuel Pepys? Well, he's good to read, don't you think? Even if he had served as a gangplank to my mother.

Mr Phillipps' daughter and I set up a bonfire close to the house, carting armfuls of old papers and academic journals and the odd nudie picture of my mother and my English teacher. We threw them all into the flames. The smoke snaked up into the sky.

*

With Mr Phillipps dead, my mother had a change of attitude towards me and my family. She became more interested in contact. Following the funeral, I would ring her every Sunday morning. During each call, she still found the need to talk about how awful my father had been – adding to the thousands of times I had already heard her customary lecture. On the other hand, she would surprise me by asking about the children, about Debra, about me. Well, a little.

She also decided to proceed with the planned house in Noosa. A change of location, a new project, might help distract from her loss. My mother threw herself into supervising the construction and made the move within a year of Mr Phillipps' death. The completed house was pleasant, with a balcony on which she could sit watching the river. She made an effort to socialise, joining the local music society and exercising her long-practised skill at taking the money at the door – no freebies – her white gloves protecting her from the germs. She developed a small circle of friends.

For all that, alone in this large house, her eccentricities had room to flourish.

I visited her once in that first year, flying up to stay a couple of days. After a few hours in her company, it was clear that her germ fetish had grown more intense. The white gloves, previously worn only on external excursions, were now mandatory whenever the front door was ajar, the fabric being anxiously tugged higher and tighter as she faced the outside world.

In her own kitchen, her habits were increasingly fastidious. At dinner time, she rapidly ate three small pieces of cheese with a couple of crackers, then moved to the sink to wash her plate. She stood by the sink, waiting for me to finish eating various parts of the meal I'd cooked myself, collecting each item as soon as it was surrendered – scooping up my teaspoon when I put it down, then my tea cup, then anxiously hovering, waiting for the plate from which I'd eaten my steak, then the bowl from which I'd eaten my salad.

'Mum, I'll wash up everything after I've finished.'

'It's better to do it as you go. I'm happier not to have the mess.'

*

Her self-absorption also seemed to be intensifying. As she hovered at the sink waiting for my wine glass, I let my eyes wander the room. Above the stove, there was a black-and-white photograph, presumably taken by my father, in which she was a nineteen-year-old ingénue, smiling for the world. Over in the corner, above the kitchen table, was an enormous framed photo of her standing in front of the half-constructed Sydney Opera House, circa 1971. And propped on a side table was an image from her time at The Australian Ballet, taken on a glittering Sydney Harbour, laughing with Rudolf Nureyev.

Topping off the collection was a large oil painting, with heavy gilt frame, that showed her as a young aristocrat – arms crossed, chin tilted upwards, dressed in a cashmere twin-set and pearls, presumably caught in an idle moment before the fox hunt at her English mansion. During my childhood, my mother always had a few photos of herself mounted on the walls, but here, in the new Noosa house, the urge had been more thoroughly indulged. It was as if her home had been taken over by the Anna Phillipps Appreciation Society.

Having finally claimed victory over my wine glass, the much-pictured woman pottered around the kitchen, wiping down surfaces that didn't need wiping down. As she did so, she described her role in various local organisations.

'In the Music Society, they don't have any system for selling the tickets and keeping the money safe. They don't have anyone like me, someone who's been part of the industry.'

'That's where you can help, Mum. I'm sure they appreciate what you do.'

'No, really, I had to take over the whole thing myself.'

Her narcissism seemed wrapped up in anxiety, in a need to prove herself worthy – as an aristocrat, as a friend of Nureyev, as a person with a spotless house, as someone who knew how to run a box office better than anyone else.

I sat at her kitchen table, watching her fret and boast and clean, always in clear sight of a photograph of herself.

This, I thought, is the problem with self-love. It's so rarely reciprocated.

After dinner, we watched television together and then she asked me to 'get the teddies ready for bed'. This involved us both mounting the stairs to the smallest bedroom. It was home to about twenty-five teddy bears, some of whose glimmering orange eyes I remembered from the hobbit hole in Armidale. They were of various shapes and sizes. Some were grouped together on a single rocking chair; others lolled on their own custom-made furniture. My mother stood in the doorway and pointed to a pile of woollen rugs.

'They like being snug for the night.'

I placed a tartan rug over the group sharing the rocking chair, tucking in the sides. There were some smaller rugs and these I placed on various furry laps.

'Keep the lamp on,' said my mother when I went to turn it off. 'They prefer a bit of light.'

*

If my mother's germ phobia was becoming more intense, so was her spirit of reinvention. The next day, I noticed a stack of mail on the desk in the kitchen. Most of the envelopes were addressed to Dr Anna Phillipps. She must have decided, following her husband's death, that his doctorate was an inheritable honour. She'd also had it included on her letterhead.

A typed curriculum vitae, copies of which she had stacked on the desk, presented what she now regarded as her background. The girl who, in reality, had left school at fourteen, in about 1938, had been transformed into a new woman.

Her CV now began:

1938–50 Educated at The Convent of Notre Dame, Yorkshire, England.

The dates given in this entry, I should explain, imply that my mother didn't leave school until she was twenty-six. Or that, miraculously, she'd been born eight years later than the date on her birth certificate.

Next up:

1951–54 Trained as a journalist with the *Yorkshire Morning Post*.

Of course, by 1954 she'd been in Australia and New Guinea for eight years, but that chunk of her life disappears. According to her CV, she was still in Yorkshire, serving as a cadet reporter.

Then the New Guinea move finally comes, six years later than in reality:

1954–58 Played a major multi-faceted role in the establishment
of Papua New Guinea's first newspaper.

It's a highly unusual case of someone transferring directly from a newspaper in the north of England to one in Papua New Guinea, with no Australian interregnum.

I don't want to sound mean. The desire to shave eight years off your age is, I know, a common one, and probably sensible if you want to remain on committees and boards once you've retired. I'm more confused about why she thought Yorkshire was better than Lancashire; about why she invented a convent school, even though she was never a Catholic; and why she shrank her adventurous twelve years in Papua New Guinea to just four – seemingly with no point other than to fit in a pretend cadetship on a regional British paper.

As often with my mother, I found her real story so much more impressive than the one she concocted.

*

My mother's spirit of perpetual reinvention also involved plastic surgery. My father, after their marriage break-up, would complain to me about the financial cost of my mother's constant desire to go under the knife. According to him, she was an early adopter.

It started when we were about to leave Sydney: when I was eleven and she was forty-five. This was in the late 1960s, when such things were not common. She was film-star good-looking, so the facelifts were odd – a continuation of the remaking of self that had seen her change name, country, social class and now her appearance.

Even in Noosa, all these decades on, the plastic surgery was clearly being topped up. Later, I found some of the receipts. Occasionally, as my mother moved around the house, cleaning and tidying, I could see the marks on the side of her face where the latest tightening had occurred. The sight of these scars always made me feel tender towards her. Surely at some point a person could stop caring so intensely about what was thought by the rest of the world?

*

That night, my final night in Noosa, we went for dinner to the local RSL club. I was to meet my mother's friends. There were three couples, one with a grown-up daughter in tow. They were all kindly, smart people, friendly towards my mother.

When the time came to choose our meals, my mother made a great show of not accepting a menu. 'They know me here,' she told me in a loud stage whisper. 'They know I just have a tiny bit of fish.'

The waiter returned and started taking orders. As each person spoke – 'I'll have the steak'; 'The Chicken Parmigiana and chips, thanks' – my mother would clap her hands together in dismay: 'I don't know how you can possibly eat all of that!' Or, 'Oh no, not sausages!' Or, 'I couldn't stand ordering that.'

When the waiter arrived at her side, she smiled primly and said, 'Just my usual,' to which the waiter nodded his understanding. My mother smiled at me, keen for me to notice how special she was, how different from her friends.

A little later, the waiter duly brought her a small portion of grilled fish with some lettuce on the side. She smiled her assent. The delivery of everyone else's meal, however, was accompanied by loud groaning from my mother: 'Look how many chips!' 'How are you going to fit it all in!' 'Really, I don't know how you do it.'

After we'd eaten, we stood around outside the club, chatting. Everyone was in a good mood, despite my mother's criticism of their food choices. The thirty-something daughter of her friends, trying to be pleasant, complimented my mother on her shoes, which were low-heeled yet brightly patterned.

The thirty-something daughter was herself wearing an attractive pair of high heels.

'I don't know how you can wear those,' my mother replied, pointing to the offending footwear. 'Only shopgirls wear high heels.'

The high-heeled daughter looked at my mother in some disbelief and then glanced at her own mother – searching for some possible explanation of why on earth anybody would put up with someone like this. Her mother smiled in that apologetic 'I know, but please don't make a fuss' way.

I did quite intensely dislike my mother at this moment – the way she acted so superior to good people who were just trying to have dinner with friends. As we drove off, I wondered how they endured her.

I presume they simply forgave her rudeness, thinking it a sad consequence of her aristocratic birth.

Chapter Ten

After a couple of years of dutiful phone calls and a few more solo visits, I decided to drive up to Noosa with Debra and the children: a repeat of the trip years before when I took Debra to visit the Enchanted Girdle. Ever since the death of Mr Phillipps, my mother had been asking more about the children and their activities. Maybe she could at last take pleasure in our family. It seemed worth a try.

It was a long drive, spread over two days, and we rolled into Noosa just after dinner. As we approached my mother's house, I counselled the children that they should refer to their grandmother by her latest chosen name – 'Anna' – avoiding the use of terms such as Nanna, or Grandmother, or Gran. My mother had long insisted she couldn't accept being called a grandmother, as she was 'far too young to be one'. Birthday cards to the children, if they arrived at all, were always signed 'From your daddy's mummy', or 'From your father's mother'.

I'm not a professor of linguistics, but I'm pretty sure that someone who is 'your father's mother' might also turn out to be 'your grandmother', but it was a point I ignored when speaking to the children.

'Just call her Anna,' was my firm instruction to those in the back seat.

We knocked on the door and were welcomed inside. My mother showed us into the living room, at which point we discovered we had a more immediate problem than the issue of what to call her. My mother had spread a large bed sheet in the centre of the floor. In the middle of the sheet she had installed a vinyl pouffe. Debra and I were invited to sit on the normal furniture, but the children were pointed towards what looked like a makeshift ebola control centre.

Debra looked at me. I looked at her. We both shrugged, wearily. With my mother, things just got weirder. We nodded to the children: do as she says.

'Shall I sit here, Anna?' said Dan, cautiously.

'Yes, Daniel, I've made that spot especially for you and your brother.'

So the two of them – Dan aged seven, Joe aged three – sat on the pouffe, itself an island in a sea of sheet.

I presume my mother was worried that her grandsons would shed germs and dirt on her furniture and carpet, much like moulting dogs. If they sat on the pouffe, she could wipe down the vinyl with disinfectant, then gather up the bed sheet, complete with whatever skin cells they had shed, and put it through the washing machine, the dial turned to 'hot'.

Was she now so mad, so clearly suffering from obsessive compulsive disorder, that I should have been a bit more sympathetic? Maybe. A nicer person would have been so. But all my focus was on my two admirable sons, who were politely complying with the commands of this strange, shrill woman.

I watched as they dutifully sat there, back to back, their faces serious and wary, like tiny Mexican bandits about to commence a duel. My mother put on the television to entertain them, but the pouffe was too small for them to sit side by side, so Dan shifted to allow his little brother to see the screen. For the next half-hour, Joe watched TV, leaning against his big brother's back, while the big brother stared patiently in the wrong direction at the blank white wall.

*

When the program finished, my mother offered to show us the room where we'd be sleeping. Dan, relieved to be released from the Centre for Disease Control, leapt up the steps. Young Joe followed, his arm darting out to steady himself against the wall.

I heard a distressed intake of breath from my mother. She leaned down to her grandson in order to address him directly.

'Now, Joseph, you mustn't touch the wall. If you touch the wall, you'll leave a mark. Then Anna will have to get the whole wall repainted. And I don't have enough money to do that.'

My mother ended the sentence with a little fake sob, underlining the gravity of the situation, as if poverty, starvation and a Dickensian workhouse were just one handprint away. My three-year-old was being invited into a detailed consideration of my mother's finances, the questionable durability of wash-and-wear paints, and the exorbitant rates charged by Queensland house-painters.

He flashed her a look. It was as close as a three-year-old could get to: 'Man, oh man, you are one crazy lady.'

*

Debra, for obvious reasons, volunteered to put the children to bed while I joined my mother in the living room. She offered me a beer and asked that I prepare her a Campari and soda. Once we were sitting comfortably, she searched around for a suitable topic of conversation. It took her three seconds.

'What are you doing about your weight problem?' she said.

'I don't have a weight problem,' I answered, somewhat aggressively, perhaps tired by the drive.

'I think you do,' my mother chirped, in the manner of a woman uttering a mischievous witticism.

'Well, maybe a kilo or two,' I replied sullenly, 'but it's none of your business.'

I took a defiant swig of my beer.

'I wouldn't normally say anything, darling,' my mother continued, 'but it's a health issue.'

This was an exaggeration. Even on official guidelines I was perhaps eight kilos overweight; I was not at death's door. Like many people, I was a victim of the food pyramid – a government-sponsored program that instructed people to eat vast quantities of pasta and rice, a policy that resulted in us taking on the shape of a pyramid.

To change the topic, I showed my mother some photographs of a block of scrub Debra and I had bought a few hours from Sydney with our old friend Philip. We were in the process of building a mud-brick house, using our own labour. One of the photos showed Debra, looking beautiful as she stood in front of a very large termite mound. The mound was a couple of metres high and a good metre wide.

'Oh, look at the size of that ant-heap,' my mother observed. 'It's almost as big as Debra.'

As was often the case with my mother, I found myself thinking, *She can't have said* that. *No way could she have implied that my attractive partner looked like an enormous pile of termite excrement.* I felt my temperature rise. If only Mr Phillipps were here he could've grabbed Mr Toad and forced a change of topic. 'I don't think anyone has noticed my fine waistcoat ...'

I told my mother that I needed to fetch the rest of the bags from our car. While passing down the hallway, I noticed she had two photographs of me on the table inside the front door. They were side by side. There was one of me at fourteen, looking painfully thin. And another, taken more recently, in which I was photographed from below in a way that made me look like Marlon Brando after eating a whale.

Whispering in our upstairs bedroom later that night, I told Debra about the twinned photos: one thin, one fat. She rolled her eyes, and presented her analysis: 'It's her way of saying, "This is him when I looked after him; and here he is under the regime of that fat girlfriend of his."'

It was an analysis hard to dispute.

*

By breakfast the next morning, I was seriously regretting the trip, much as I had regretted the visit to the hobbit hole all those years before. Feeding the children their toast and cereal while my mother hovered with rubber-gloved hands involved more tension than I'd ever experienced before – at least in the period before I'd eaten my own breakfast. I'd also woken with a cold, which I knew my mother saw as a sign of weakness and loose living.

'I don't know what you've been doing that you have a cold,' she said as she looked lovingly at the sink.

'It's just one of those things, Mum. Chance. Nothing else,' I replied as I spread Vegemite onto Joe's toast.

'Well,' she said, 'I've never had a cold. Never in my whole life have I had a cold. And my teeth are perfect. I went to the dentist last week and he said, "Anna, I don't know why you bother to come. Your teeth are perfect."'

'That's very lucky, Mum.'

'It's not luck. It's care.'

She nodded vigorously, indicating the enthusiasm with which she agreed with herself. After that, she washed three plates, just to celebrate.

*

My mother had always held the view that ill health was a sign of moral decay and misbehaviour. Being sick deserved no sympathy and certainly no treatment. Doctors – aside from plastic surgeons, I suppose – were the problem rather than the solution. These views were held so firmly they even survived the manifestly undeserved death of Mr Phillipps. Maybe she saw his sickness as the exception that proved the rule.

In all other cases, illness was caused by indulgence in undisciplined lower-class practices. These included:

- eating garlic;
- going outside with your hands exposed, rather than encased in white cotton gloves;
- walking around in thongs;
- ordering from the menu at restaurants instead of asking for 'just a little bit of fish';
- being fat;
- being common;
- eating hot chips.

If, in my phone calls to her, I reported a visit to a doctor, she'd become instantly concerned.

'What? You went to a *doctor*?'

There'd be an incredulous pause on the other end of the phone.

'Well, no wonder you're sick.'

*

Even apart from my cold, the visit was turning into a disaster. I'd wanted my mother to properly know her grandchildren, yet she remained so uncomfortable and anxious that it was impossible for them to form any connection. The children treated her as you would a madman wired with explosives. They were polite but enormously wary. Debra tried to jolly everyone along, especially me, but I could see she was tiring of the task.

After breakfast I suggested a trip to the beach. My mother, surprisingly, said she would accompany us. She drove us there in her car, but, once arrived, she refused to step onto the sand. Instead she stood on the concrete path, her white gloves pulled tight, guarding our kicked-off shoes. We had a quick swim and returned to find that she'd been busy with our footwear. All four pairs of shoes were now in an orderly row, largest to smallest, the laces splayed outwards in a neat pattern.

Love is a difficult thing to express and everyone has to do it in their own way. Perhaps, in those neatly arranged shoes, largest to smallest, my mother was showing her affection in the only way possible.

All the same, by the time we'd arrived back at the house, I had a strong sense that Alice/Bunty/Anna wanted us to move on. For a start, she'd spent the drive making promises to the car that it would be thoroughly cleaned once we removed our slightly sandy limbs.

'How long are you staying?' she asked over dinner that night in a tone of voice that carried an edge of panic.

I paused, already realising that we'd never survive the length of visit we'd planned, four whole days – a period which now seemed geological in length.

'Well,' I said, 'we were planning to go back on Friday morning, but it is a very long drive …'

'Oh, yes, darling,' my mother said, seizing the opportunity, 'it's a veeeeeery long drive.'

'So,' I continued, 'maybe we need to leave on Thursday morning or maybe even tomorrow evening.'

My mother nodded, as if she had been newly apprised of the distance between Noosa and Sydney. 'Yes. It. Is. A. Very. Long. Drive,' she repeated, hitting each word in turn.

'So,' I said, keen to accept the hint, 'best we go back tomorrow, maybe mid-morning so we can get a good start.'

Our stay had been cut in half, just as our trip to the hobbit hole had been halved all those years before.

And, once again, it was to the immense relief of all combatants.

*

Six months later my mother rang and announced that she planned to stay with us for the night. She was in Sydney for an arts meeting and needed accommodation. You'll think I'm being unpleasant if I claim she only stayed with us because she was horrified at the cost of Sydney hotels, so let me put it this way: Sydney hotels are very expensive.

A maternal visit was an alarming prospect and made me want to give the place a thorough scrubbing. I was keen to avoid a repeat of the incident in which my mother had taken a pump pack of Spray n'Wipe and cleaned our stove-top to death. I was also aware that she'd have an opinion on the size of the elephant in the room, the one named Richard. And so, prior to her arrival, I cleaned and I dieted – annoyed all the while that I cared so much about the opinion of someone with so little interest in me.

Debra offered to assist with the big clean-up, but I waved her away. 'She's my mother,' I said as I scrubbed at the sink, 'so it's my problem.'

But Debra shook her head. 'We're in this together. Besides, the woman always gets the blame.'

I said to Debra, 'Why should you be responsible for her opinion about the house, or about me being fat. It's nothing to do with you. You shouldn't care what she thinks.'

Debra shrugged, wearily, as she walked past me to the laundry, returning with a bucket of cleaning gear. She knelt on the kitchen floor, squirted some Jiff onto her cloth, and started scouring a recalcitrant skirting board. As she cleaned she started singing – I imagine for comic purposes. It was a mournful slave song from the American South. She was hopeful, it seemed, that some sort of chariot might swing low and take her to heaven.

Swing low, sweet chariot
Coming for to carry me home …

I moved on to the back yard, polishing the sides of the barbecue and squirting window cleaner onto the glass doors. I could see Debra moving around the kitchen, scrubbing out various cupboards. By now she was singing 'Let My People Go' in a yearning alto.

Oh, let us all from bondage flee,
Let my people go!

Amusing? Well, up to a point.

I tackled the bathroom, washing the ceiling with sugar soap, causing streams of caustic chemicals to splash directly onto my face. On the upside, I was sweating so much I just had to be losing weight. Debra, meanwhile, was now in the laundry, collecting all the disinfectants and detergents.

She marched past me, carrying a large box. 'When your father visited we had to hide all the grog,' she observed. 'Now your mother's visiting, we have to hide all the cleaning products.'

I moved on to the boys' bedrooms, while Debra got busy in the lounge room. As I moved past, I could see she was spraying the dog with air-freshener. I could hear her singing *Death be my friend and take me to my lord.*

Or something like that. OK, quite funny.

*

Three days later, my mother knocked on our door and I showed her in. She was wearing what she called her 'travel suit' – a tweed skirt and jacket, with contrast trim, stiff and fitted like armour. Her hair was pulled into a tight, fierce bun; her face was powdered with make-up. As she walked up the hallway I could see her usual reflex of anxiety – pulling her gloves on a little tighter. Onto the kitchen table she unpacked all her food for the visit: small amounts of cheese and crispbread and some home-made muesli, all of it in a series of small Tupperware boxes. 'I don't really eat anything at all,' she said yet again, 'really nothing at all.'

I showed her around the house. She admired Dan's bedroom, with its collection of soccer trophies, and observed that Debra was a 'natural mother'. This, I'm pretty sure, was my mother's codeword for 'fat'. I took pleasure in the fact that, as yet, she'd said nothing about me.

We went for a walk, me slightly ahead with the two boys, while Debra followed with my mother. I could feel my mother's eyes on me as I pushed up the hill. She was battling with herself about whether to say anything, anything at all, and, to be fair to my mother, she managed to restrict herself to just one small point of disappointment.

'You know,' my mother said to Debra, 'he used to be taller.'

*

The next morning we asked my mother to look after Joe while we took his older brother to school. All she needed to do was sit him in front of the TV and supply him with some Vegemite toast. While we were away, she put the toast in front of him, left the room, then came back five minutes later to find the toast untouched. She reproached him in her usual posh accent: 'You haven't eaten your toast. You must do it now. Otherwise I'll get into trouble with your daddy and I'll cry and cry.'

It may seem odd that I can report her dialogue with such accuracy, but she later recounted the whole scene to me, playing her own part with some vigour. According to her own account, she left the room for another five minutes, came back and checked again. 'Oh, good boy, you've eaten your toast.'

Joe, who by now had turned four, looked up at her and said calmly, 'I haven't eaten it, I've hidden it. I want you to get into trouble with Daddy.'

For a woman with a germ phobia, the hidden breakfast was not good news. Somewhere in the room was the Vegemite toast, sending out its greasy germs and buttery spores into the air. My mother became frantic. My tiny son would not help, refusing to say where he had hidden it. She was on her hands and knees, pulling aside couch cushions, peering under rugs, hyperventilating as she tried to find the toast. We came home to find her still crawling around the room: hair astray, stricken, pale. She left for her meeting soon after, a broken woman.

Once she'd gone, I asked, 'What did you do with the toast, Joe?'

My boy wandered over to the stereo system and retrieved the toast from behind a speaker. He let flash a tiny triumphant smile. I frowned at him while secretly cheering him on.

Throughout my life, I'd never been much of a match for my mother. But I'd had a role in bringing into life someone who was.

Chapter Eleven

With my mother alone in Noosa, my father was increasingly alone in Sydney. After the mishap of falling off his boat and sundry other disasters, Robyn had thrown him out yet again, although their relationship seemed to limp on. He was living in a downbeat apartment in Bondi, his funds having been exhausted by too many wives, too many boats and too many houses. His drinking had resulted in a clutch of medical problems which saw him regularly hospitalised.

Despite all this, I wanted to maintain a connection, if only to avoid the guilt of the inattentive son. Unlike my mother, my father seemed to enjoy being with my children, on the rare occasions he saw them. Hoping to build on this, I'd offer to pick him up and take him to watch his grandsons play soccer, the game of his youth. Sometimes he'd agree, but mostly he seemed reluctant. Whether it was the cold winds of the soccer field or the way it would eat into valuable Saturday-morning drinking time,

I'm uncertain, but I found the reluctance annoying. Despite good grandparents on Debra's side, my boys were still hungry for family. On the rare occasions my father turned up for soccer, they were thrilled. His lack of interest in them reminded me of his lack of interest in me.

To be fair, he had become darkly depressed. He'd ring Debra, working in her home office, and talk about his despair. On one occasion he claimed to be preparing to commit suicide as she listened. 'I've got the pills lined up. Give me one reason not to take them.'

Debra replied, 'Give me a minute, Ted.'

Actually, she didn't say that, although she confessed to the urge when she told me the story. In reality, she talked to him for an hour about his grandchildren – how they'd miss him and the way he wouldn't see them growing up.

Later that night, she reminisced about a day when my father had been in hospital and we'd taken Joe and Dan to visit. Ted's eyes had lit up when the two boys came into his room. Joe had performed a little dance by Ted's bedside in order to cheer him up – doing twirls and jumps and ridiculous bows. Dan – older, more serious – read aloud a piece he'd written that had just won a short story prize for young writers. As Debra recounted the details, she became teary. 'That day, when I saw the pleasure in his eyes, it was so awful to think what he'd missed out on, of how he could have been a grandfather to them, of what he could have meant to them. I remember when Joe danced, Ted said, "I can't take my eyes off him," and I thought, "You know, Ted, you never had to take your eyes off him. No one required it of you.'"

In the course of telling me about my father's phone call, Debra had gone from a glib Jocasta-like joke about the would-be suicide to deep sadness about my parents – the proper paternal grandparents our children had been denied, and the way they'd missed out themselves on the experience of getting to know our two fabulous boys.

It was a shift in emotions I found familiar. I'd often experienced it when talking about my mother and father: I'd be jokey, then maudlin, then a bit pissed off. It was hard to stare at them full on; they needed to be held at arm's length. The disappointment I sometimes felt could only be defused by considering them as a comic tale, a ripping yarn, a bundle of eccentricities.

And yet there was an undertow of sadness which I did my best to ignore.

*

Ted's last year was marked by the kindness of strangers. I'd receive phone calls after he'd collapsed in the street or become miserable in a bar. People looked after him. He'd give them my phone number and they'd call. They'd report his latest drama like it was fresh news, a problem that had surely never occurred before.

'He's fallen over in the street. I hate to say this, but he may have drunk a little too much.'

'Your father is in our restaurant. He's become quite upset. I think his wife has just left him; is that right?'

'He says everyone is trying to crucify him. I think he must have had some really bad news.'

I appreciated their optimism – that here was a good man, a man who had taken a single, and recent, tumble.

Then one night, late, the phone rang and a doctor said my father was in hospital and might not make it through the night. He was seventy-five. I drove to the Prince of Wales Hospital in Sydney's Randwick and walked into the ward. My father was unconscious on the bed, his body large with fluid. He'd had what the doctors called an upper gastrointestinal tract haemorrhage. I sat with him through the night and was there when he died in the early hours. The cause of death was a haemorrhage due to cirrhosis of the liver – his blood was flowing out of his oesophageal varices into the rest of his body. According to the medical certificate his blood-alcohol level at the time of death was .2, a level at which, I discovered later, 'you need help to stand or walk and at which blackouts are likely'. Who knew that the cause-of-death certificate would be such an unforgiving document, such a clear inventory of one's sins?

I was working on radio by then, presenting a program in the late afternoon, which meant arriving at the office at about 11am. It never occurred to me not to go to work. Although it seems strange to me now, I turned up as normal. A few hours after my father's death, I was reading out the traffic and interviewing politicians. I do remember crying just before I went on air. My friend Philip was working at the station and he walked over and cradled me as I stood in the middle of the office, suddenly sobbing. Selfish, I know, but I wasn't really crying for my father. I was crying for the yearned-for parent I didn't receive, but whom we all feel we deserve.

*

While I was on the radio, Debra rang my mother to tell her the news. My mother sighed knowingly and blamed – accurately, but unfeelingly – my father's drinking. Debra talked about the funeral, which we'd now have to plan, asking if my mother would want to attend. My mother responded by introducing the subject of Mr Phillipps' funeral – describing in detail the large cathedral in Armidale and how many hundreds of people had attended, listing their names with little squeals of triumph. 'Well,' my mother concluded with a hoot, 'it won't be like that for Ted. I can't think who will come.'

When I arrived home, Debra described the phone call, and how she found herself holding the phone at a distance from her ear so as not to be too close to my mother's glee.

'I felt protective of your father,' Debra said, surprising herself. She then gave me a tough look. 'She can only come to the funeral if she agrees not to badmouth him.'

I rang my mother and set the terms of her attendance at my father's funeral: no comparisons with Mr Phillipps, no criticising Ted to his grandchildren, no comments on the paucity of mourners. My mother signalled her agreement with a querulous snort, indicating that she was bravely bearing the weight of some unreasonable demands.

In the event, eleven of us attended my father's funeral. His old friend Steve Stephens had already died, so the funeral party consisted of me, Debra, our two sons, my mother, Debra's father, Max, and our friend Amanda, as well as Ted's final estranged partner, Robyn, a single old friend of my father's from Canberra and two chaps from Bowral.

I gave the eulogy. I talked about my dad's achievements, his adventurous character and the fact that he'd lost his way. I told a story that seemed to sum up his best side: when I was seventeen, there was an arts festival in Canberra called Australia '75. I spotted a notice appealing for last-minute accommodation: it was for a group of twelve indigenous dancers, travelling down from the Northern Territory. I asked my father if we could put them up in our suburban home and the answer came straight away: 'Of course we can. That would be *great.*' I spent the week living at the festival, sleeping in a tent with my friends, while my father enthusiastically hosted the indigenous dancers, cooking them breakfast in the mornings and sharing beers at night. It was a measure of his gregarious spirit.

After the funeral I received condolence letters from a handful of my father's acquaintances, all of whom found different ways to say the same thing. Here's one: 'As a young man he was wonderful fun and a great journalist and we admired him very much. It's a shame that he seemed to drift away from all that later on.' And another: 'In the early days of the *South Pacific Post*, Ted was an excellent boss and a very good friend. I didn't have much to do with him in recent years, but I'll always remember him.'

At lunch my mother tried to talk to Debra about how terrible Ted had been and I saw the way Debra's mouth tightened out of loyalty to my dad. At the other end of the table, the old friend of my father sat next to eleven-year-old Dan and told him stories of his grandfather and what a fine man he'd been. I listened in, my throat tightening in gratitude.

*

Next there was the job of cleaning out my father's flat. Not much was left of what Debra and I used to call 'Lord Ted' – the ebullient Lord of the Manor, dispensing hospitality and generosity, his wallet initially full and then happily emptying. The expensive paintings which used to line the Gallery – the hallway of our Canberra house – were all long gone. The furniture had been reduced by a series of relocations to ever smaller accommodation. I saved his personal papers and a few New Guinea artefacts – some spears and ceremonial walking sticks and three side-tables, each carved from a slice of log. I encouraged Robyn to take the paintings she'd particularly liked. A second-hand dealer came and offered $400 for the rest. Robyn and I accepted.

At home, I packed the papers away. A good proportion of the collection consisted of letters from my mother. One was her reply to a condolence letter my father had sent following Mr Phillipps' death, in which she described her second husband's funeral:

Dear Teddy. My sincere thanks for your letter of sympathy. The whole business has been a terrible shock, he was such a superbly fit man, neither smoked nor drank, played first-class sport; one would have thought he would outlive us all. I must say the support of all our friends has been my greatest comfort. I have just written my 183rd thank you! I must say that the longer I knew him, the more I appreciated his fine qualities. The end of him is, indeed, the end of my life.

She signed off with the hope that my father was happy and well, and then attached an article from the university staff newsletter detailing Mr Phillipps' professional achievements plus the order of service from the funeral, showing the participation of the university's Deputy Vice-Chancellor.

It's uncertain how happy and well my father felt after receiving her 'thanks', the whole thing a coded way of saying 'Why, oh why, didn't you die instead of him?'

I flipped through the rest of her letters to my father. They were nearly all about money and her deep unhappiness about the settlement she was given at the time of their divorce. In several different letters, written over many years, she insisted that Mr Phillipps had no share of the hobbit hole house. For my father to give extra funds to her, she argued, would not be giving money to him. She detailed her loans and the low value of her assets. In other letters, again sent over a number of years, she detailed her thrift: 'I never go to a restaurant, I never have my hair done.'

About a decade and a half after the divorce, she was still writing to Ted:

I do feel very bitter, there is no doubt I got a raw deal out of our twenty-seven years, I know you say I haven't, but who is the one living in a superb house with cars and another house bringing in rent, and even after that, money invested to give you income? I didn't even manage to save a penny of the rather poor wages I got for standing untold hours in the newsagency ... please don't do what you did last time and ignore my appeal, I really need help from the only person that I feel able, and indeed should be able, to go to.

It was unclear whether my father had sent money, just as it was unclear whether she was right or wrong about the poor deal she'd been given. All I could see was that Ted had covered the typed note in angry doodles.

As I looked at the pile of begging letters, I started to turn around some shards of memory. In particular: my mother's strange present-giving. Her gifts to me on the occasion of Christmas and my birthday formed part of my arsenal of stories when playing Who's Got the Weirdest Parents?. Her birthday presents were parsimonious bordering on the hilarious. One year she rang and asked what I'd like for my birthday; I suggested a picnic set, having in mind one of those wicker baskets, with a set of plastic plates, cups and cutlery, all held in place with fake-leather straps. They were relatively cheap and easy to buy. A week later, the postman delivered my gift. My mother had somehow located a second-hand Globite school suitcase, scuffed and stained, into which she'd placed four used plastic plates, all of them heavily knife-scored, a handful of old metal cutlery, thrown in loose, and four chipped china mugs.

For years I'd told the story as a bit of fun, a tale of a tightwad mother with short arms and long pockets. Now, with her letters to my father spread out before me, I saw the picnic basket in less comic terms. It was a cry of rage, really; her way of expressing how tough she was doing it and her anger towards the child who'd sprung from such a financially ruinous union. As suitcases go, that Globite really did represent baggage.

*

After my father's death, I'd been in contact with his relatives in England, sending them details of his funeral service. It reminded me that I still knew nothing of the family on my mother's side. For over twenty years I'd known her accent was a fake and her childhood was an invention. I'd told the truth to my children – I didn't want them thinking they came from 'posh stock' – and yet I'd cautioned them about ever saying anything to her. What was the point in challenging her fabulous fantasy of being an only child born to English aristocrats? All the same, it would be worth five minutes of my time to find out a little more.

By the early 2000s genealogy websites were becoming popular on the internet. All those years before, when my aunt had revealed the truth about my mother's family, she'd told me the names of my mother's two sisters: Bertha and Molly. I also, of course, knew my mother's maiden name: Sudall. With this information in hand, I logged onto a genealogy website. It was Christmas time and my mother had accepted an invitation to mark the occasion with us. She would arrive in a few days' time, trilling her upper-class tones: what fun to know more of the truth before she arrived, even while realising I'd never do anything with the information.

I typed in the names and within about a minute had surprised myself by finding the Sudall family tree. The three daughters were there, alongside their parents: Harold and Annie. Detailed information would be harder to find, but here were the basics. My son Joe, now eight years old, was walking past my bedroom as I typed. I gestured him in, showing him the outline and the names. He smiled. It was the same evil smile that he'd given, four years earlier, when he'd hidden the Vegemite toast.

'We should print out the family tree,' he said. He was using hand movements, showing the sheet coming out of the printer. 'Then we could laminate it.' More hand gestures. 'Then use it as the place-mat for Christmas lunch.' He mimed showing my mother to her seat and pointing to her place-mat: 'Good news, Nanna Anna, we've found your family.'

I ignored this gloriously wicked idea, while enjoying his disruptive spirit. I did, however, print off the details of my mother's clandestine family. One day, when I could be bothered, I'd dedicate myself to the task of finding the truth. Could it be there was more to my mother's story than the desire to escape her social class? Was there something else about her parents that made her want to reinvent herself?

I had an urge to find out. Then again, I also had an urge to leave the whole thing alone. When you have a thorn in your foot, is it better to try to get it out, rooting around with a needle, causing all sorts of pain, or should you just leave it alone, hoping it will be expelled over time? As I mucked around on the internet I realised I didn't have an answer to that.

Chapter Twelve

My mother had become increasingly fearful of crime so, eight years after her move to Noosa, she sold her house and bought a block of land, a few kilometres away, inside a 'gated community' – a development with about forty blocks inside a perimeter fence. She had her budget-conscious Armidale builder – the one who'd built both Doriath and her first Noosa house – construct a new place to her design. The concept was eccentric. It was a standard rectangular house into which a large swimming pool had been plonked, right in the middle of things, with nothing but a low glass fence separating the water from the formal sitting room and dining room. It looked as odd as it sounds: there was the pool, a metre of tiling, the low glass fence and then carpeting, upon which was arranged a collection of immensely formal pieces of furniture, including grandfather clocks, early Victorian chairs and a French-polished dining-room table. It was as if a Florida beach house had been picked up by a tornado then crash-landed into the middle of an eighteenth-century English mansion.

Nearly all the rooms overlooked the pool, the main exception being a cosy study, which featured a built-in bookshelf and tiny chairs occupied by the teddy bears. The room was a memorial to Mr Phillipps: the bears they'd shared, seated in the usual semi-circle, ready to watch the television; his collection of model cars in a display cabinet; and then his books, filling every wall – hardback editions of Tolkien, CS Lewis and, yes, Samuel Pepys.

I would visit once or twice a year – mostly for just a day or two, and always on my own, in order to save the children and Debra further pain. The bears and the library were at the centre of life in the house. If we were leaving to go to the shops, my mother would stand at the door of the study and speak to the bears. 'Richard and I are about to go out. So will you fellows please look after everything?'

Last thing at night, she'd give me the task of preparing the bears for sleep, just as she'd done in the last house, requiring me to move around the circle of stuffed toys, placing a small blanket over each furry lap. I was then required to say, 'Goodnight, fellows,' before closing the door.

The bears, the books and the furniture became a fresh source of anxiety for my mother: what would happen to them after she was gone? She asked me to pledge that I would never sell the house or the furniture. Her belief was that, following her death, Debra and I would move to Noosa and live among her things. She seemed especially distraught at the idea that her various collections might be broken up, and fearful that her friends might somehow get in and steal items they had previously admired. I'm sure she'd never read *Zorba the Greek*, but she seemed to be channelling the macabre scene in which the villagers, like black crows, strip clean the house of the newly dead widow:

> Old women, men, children went rushing through the doors, jumped through the open windows, over the fences and off the balcony, each carrying whatever he had been able to snatch … poor old Uncle Anagnosti went about shouting, begging the people to stop, waving his stick at them.

Her preoccupation with mortality was not limited to her possessions. Around this time she also made arrangements with the local funeral director and cemetery, reserving a plot for herself. I realise this is not uncommon. Less common: she also purchased a gravestone. She had it engraved with her name and then installed in the local Noosa cemetery. As soon as it was erected, she sent me a photo: a photo of her completed grave. There was the headstone, with her name on it, and also in place the granite slab which completed the job. If you walked past in Noosa Cemetery, you'd assume she was already dead and buried.

I feel I should include a copy of the receipt, since I'm sure you'll think I'm making all this up.

Tax Invoice

Ref No: S 07

Cemetery: Tewantin

Description of memorial:
For the construction of a single grey granite memorial.

Material & labour	$5 800.00	
GST	$ 580.00	
Total cost	$6 380.00	PAID In Full

Admittedly, the gravestone was a bit light on information: there was no date or place of birth, both of which she wanted to keep secret, nor a date of death, which was hardly surprising since it had yet to occur. There was, however, a standard poetic verse: *Weep not for me though I am gone.*

To go with the grave, she purchased an American coffin. It cost $6900 and she had it delivered to her home. The coffin was placed upright in the back of her garage, still in its cardboard box, with the name of the model printed on the side: 'The Batesville Golden Pearl Casket'. It had been imported from the United States to match her special requirements: that the coffin be made of stainless steel so that her body would last as long as possible; and that it be extra-wide so that the teddies could be arranged on either side of her.

'They argue among themselves,' she'd often say during our phone calls, 'about who will be the closest to me in the coffin.'

*

My mother's neighbours had become worried about her and rang me. She'd developed what they considered an odd friendship with an unlikely man. He was about thirty years her junior. They would go to dinner each night at a local pub, the sort of establishment she would have previously labelled 'dirty' and 'common'. They would drink and eat. She would pay.

I rang my mother and explained everyone's concern.

'It doesn't seem right, Mum. I think you should be careful.'

'He takes me walking. I'm lonely and he takes me walking.'

She'd always liked male attention, the thrill of turning heads when she walked into a room, and perhaps this was her last hurrah. I commenced a long series of heated conversations with my mother, asking her about this man. Who was he? What was he up to?

'Mum, all your friends are worried. It really is a bit weird. I'm worried about you. I'd like you to say you'll stop seeing him. Can you promise me that you'll stop seeing him?'

'Yes,' my mother would say, 'I'll stop seeing him.'

The next night, someone would call me to say she was back with him, usually in the local pub.

My calls became longer, louder, more frustrating. I would stand in my bedroom at home, shouting into the phone.

'You are in danger. Don't you understand? Mum, you promised me ...'

One moment she would seem to agree with me. Then a minute later she would be talking about how she wanted to catch up with him again straight away. I would bellow some more, frustrated that I couldn't get through to her. Maybe she was right to ignore me; maybe the man was just being friendly.

The neighbour, though, was sufficiently worried to contact the police. A young constable went to the house and, although he couldn't do anything official, warned the man he was being watched. It made no difference. A few weeks on, it was New Year's Eve. The police were called again. This time my mother had been found unconscious, lying on the pavement some distance from the house. She was treated by ambulance officers and carried home. A young police officer, Jason, called me and said they suspected she may have been drugged. They'd found the man inside the house, watching television.

Jason went to visit my mother a week later. He rang me to describe the conversation. He'd talked to my mother about his suspicions. He told her he thought it possible the man was trying to prove they were in a relationship so that, later on, he could demand a share of her assets. My mother said, 'Yes, but Jason, I'm lonely.' Jason told her about his own early years, when he'd found it difficult to find a girlfriend: 'I was lonely too, Anna, so I understand what that feels like.'

Listening to this, I had to keep reminding myself I was talking to a member of the Queensland Police Force, once thought to be the toughest, most venal in the country. I said to him, 'Jason, it's very kind of you to spend so much time with my mother and talk to her so personally about yourself.'

He replied, 'Richard, it's no trouble at all. It's just modern policing.'

*

Jason put the frighteners on the man, but really there was not much he could do since my mother refused to make a complaint. My mother and I had further distressing phone calls, in which she again promised to cut off contact with the man. Sometimes within hours of her promises, I would be called by concerned locals at the pub reporting their arrival.

Then my mother fell on some paving. An ambulance was called. She was taken to hospital. Once there, she had a number of tests. She had a serious infection. And, they said, signs of dementia. Suddenly her behaviour made sense. I felt instantly guilty about our phone calls and the way I'd shouted at her for continually reneging on the promises she'd made. All through those long telephone conversations she hadn't really been able to comprehend what I was saying; certainly not enough to retain it. I felt a real beast.

The hospital refused to release her until I'd found a nursing home, which, with the help of one of my mother's friends, I did: a pleasant place with wide verandas and gardens in which she could walk. I flew up to help move her in. She seemed quite happy about it, perhaps even relieved. Living at home, while feeling her mind give way, must have made her more anxious than she'd been letting on.

Once in the nursing home, her chequebook was no longer in her possession. Almost immediately, the man lost interest, whether due to the chequebook's incapacitation or my mother's, I couldn't say. He visited twice and then never again. He made a last effort to claim possession of her car, which had been left at the local mechanic's, but the mechanic sent him on his way.

On holidays, I would fly up to Noosa and visit the nursing home. It consisted of lodges set amid well-maintained gardens. There was a walkway which took you to a large aviary, also a hall where they held Friday afternoon drinks. Residents had separate rooms, each with an en-suite bathroom, surrounding a shared dining room. This communal area could, admittedly, be a little confronting. There were so many people in a state of decline. One day I saw an old man jack-knifed into a chair with a built-in tray. He was bent forward, his nose about two inches from the tray as if his spine could no longer hold him upright. I walked a little closer, feeling heartbroken at this image of collapsed, folded-in humanity. Closer still I realised he was bent over just so he could read the tiny type of the *Guardian Weekly*, spread out on his tray. I cautioned myself against making assumptions.

My mother was more positive and relaxed than ever before.

'Is the food good?' I asked her.

'Yes, very good,' she replied.

For the first time in her life she was eating without self-denial. She wasn't worried about her appearance; the germ-defeating gloves had been thrown aside. She had her own room, with a television set she had going constantly. When I visited we'd go for long, slow walks around the grounds, with my arm hooked through hers for support.

With each visit, though, the dementia became more pronounced. On one occasion, I was copying out my journalists' contact book as a present for Dan, my older son, who'd just won his first job – following his father and grandfather into the trade. He was to be a radio announcer in Mount Isa, the outback mining town. My contact book was laid out alphabetically by topic, each person selected as an expert in their field. If you required an Astronomer, or Bat Expert, or Doctor with an Interest in Lightning, then my book could supply an instant name and number. I sat with my mother as I copied it out. It was a job which would take many hours, over a few days, so it could be perfectly combined with this pre-Christmas visit. I just had to get used to the rhythm of the conversation.

Mother: What are you doing?

Me: Writing out phone numbers for Dan. He's got his first job.

Mother: Oh.

(pause)

Mother: What are you doing?

Me: Writing out phone numbers for Dan. He's just got a job.

Mother: Oh.

(pause)

Mother: What are you doing?

Me: Writing out phone numbers for Dan. So he can use them

    in his new job.

Mother: Oh.

(pause)

And so on through the day, until the conversation, with small variations, had been repeated hundreds of times.

Each night I said goodbye to my mother at the nursing home and went back to sleep at her house, with the strange swimming pool, the teddies and the coffin. I sat there, staring at all her stuff; the leftovers of a life. I thought about renting out the house to generate some income for my mother, but where would I store all her furniture, all her papers, all the framed photographs that had been accumulated, over many years of collecting, by the Dr Anna Phillipps Appreciation Society?

And how would I explain the coffin in the garage?

*

I felt sympathy for my mother at moments like this, but then my mind would swing in a more hostile direction. I'd find myself thinking about the distance she'd always maintained between the two of us. I'd think about the time she said she'd never held me as a baby; about the way she used me as a dumping place for her hostility towards my father; about her constant, self-serving attempt to cast me as the person 'who found David', thus turning me into the author of my parents' divorce.

I compared all this to the relationship I had with my own children – imperfect in the usual ways, but always close and warm. I hoped I'd given them – by some proportion, large or small – more love than I'd received.

I know that's a big thing to claim. My fingers object to typing it. Self-doubt intrudes. All I know for sure is that this idea – giving more love than you received – has power when you see it in others.

A few years before, I'd attended the seventieth birthday party of a family friend, Noel Franks. The birthday boy was – and is – a great bloke, and father to an endless tribe of (mostly) daughters. All spoke in turn to the gathered guests; all ended up in tears.

There was one speech, if you can call it a speech, sobbed out briefly as it was, that was particularly moving. Some speakers can reduce you to tears after twenty minutes of slow build. This speaker – Noel's daughter Joanne – did it in her first, and only, sentence. 'If you knew the sort of childhood Dad had, but then what a wonderful father he was to us …'

That was it. Speaker sobbing. Speech over. Whole room reduced to tears. And in that moment it seemed like we'd been told the meaning of life: to give out more good than you'd received. Or, to put it in the negative, to pass on less shit than you'd suffered.

In the middle of this circle of love sat Noel, the birthday boy: the man who had taken darkness and turned it into light.

*

If I'm uncomfortable about claiming myself as a great parent, I'm confident in claiming Debra as one. I think of a period when Joe was fourteen. He'd been playing the harmonica for a couple of years and had developed an interest in the arcane craft of customising the instrument to suit particular playing styles. It was an esoteric task in which you'd take the factory-made object and carefully file down some of the internal parts to change the quality of the note.

The craft was so obscure there was really only one man in Australia who knew how to do it: Neil Graham, a fabulously eccentric bushman and blues player. With a background as a boilermaker and welder, he now supplied his customised instruments to professional harmonica players around the world.

Neil lives in a solar-powered house deep in the forests of the New South Wales south coast, the sort of house in which the furniture is covered in the skins of feral cats he's killed in order to help protect the native wildlife. Joe wanted to spend a week learning at Neil's feet, and Neil was happy to have an apprentice. So Debra drove Joe down and booked into a motel in the nearest town. Each day she'd drive Joe an hour into the forest and each evening drive back to pick him up again. In between trips, she'd sit in the motel room getting on with her writing. With the exception of the cat-skin chairs, it's an unremarkable story: most parents of our generation would have a version of it, dropping everything to help their children follow a passion. Yet devotion of this type would have been unimaginable for my parents and – frankly – for most of the parents of their time. Today's parents are often criticised for being too involved, fearful and child-focused. They are derided as 'helicopter parents'. They over-parent, it is said, robbing children of their selfhood.

Pandering to this fashionably negative view of today's parents, the publishing world is now full of rosy portraits of growing up in the 1950s or '60s when kids had their freedom, taking pot-shots with air rifles, whooshing down creeks on home-made rafts – the product of supposedly wise parents who understood risk and knew how to give kids the time and space to explore.

I'm sure such a childhood existed for many, but it's not my memory. I had the air rifle, that's true, and at age eight or nine I would cycle to that creek where kids had constructed a raft from old oil drums and tried to make it float. But I also remember the occasional loneliness of a '60s childhood. Many parents were simply disengaged. They didn't 'give kids their freedom'; they just weren't that interested in their role as parents. There were paedophiles in the bushes, out-of-control priests in the choir stalls and gangs in the schoolyard. And when things did go wrong, there was no culture of intimacy and trust between parent and child that allowed the child to tell and the parent to believe.

A few years ago, the Sydney Opera House staged a Festival of Dangerous Ideas, and included a speaker who attacked parents for being over-protective. It made me so mad, as this was not a 'dangerous' idea at all; it was the most conventional of ideas, a staple of a million talkback radio sessions and Facebook posts. 'When we were kids ...' The really dangerous idea had been left unspoken: that the glorious free-wheeling past of the '60s and '70s had been driven by parental apathy more than anything else.

My main memory of childhood is being alone, either sitting in my room with a book or cycling around the suburb, looking for something to do. My father was a member of the Sydney Cricket Ground and passionate about the game; he'd go regularly but never invited me. The same with golf, despite his membership of a nearby country club. I do recall the two of us playing a single game of squash when I was nine years old. It's a happy memory, but a rare one. My mother, meanwhile, would take me places – but mainly to suit her own needs. During school holidays I'd sit around her workplace – the Elizabethan Theatre Trust in Kings Cross. As a ten-year-old, I spent a lot of time either watching opera rehearsals or walking along Darlinghurst Road, ignoring the strip clubs on my way to buy a milkshake. I hope this doesn't sound like I'm whining; I'd have hated the cricket, while being exposed to both the opera and the outrages of Kings Cross was a privilege. My point is that this was typical of the time; kids were meant to bend to the convenience of their parents, whether that meant sitting through a production of Wagner, or – in other families – sitting in a stifling car outside the pub while dad downed five schooners, a lemonade handed through the car window if your father happened to recall your existence.

They were helicopter parents of a different sort – ones that constantly flew away from their children with barely a farewell wave.

*

Am I being accurate about my parents' attitude towards me? Can my sense of it be true: that these two self-obsessed people had a baby in whom they were largely uninterested? It sounds unlikely: having the child, in the circumstances described, took some effort. I know from photographs that my mother rewarded herself with a car featuring BOY numberplates, a precursor of her later numberplate celebrating Bilbo Baggins. Maybe there is a different narrative that I'm missing. Were there points at which things were normal?

I try to form the case for the defence. I remember being in bed with my mother and father when I was eight or nine, sitting between them, reading the comics as they read the Sunday papers. That sounds like a functional family. My mother would make me breakfast, involving thick slices of Vogel's bread, sawn direct from the grain-dense loaf, as was standard practice in this Amish belt of Sydney's north shore. I also remember her impromptu manicures. She was very concerned about my cuticles, and would make me sit close to her on the couch, using her own fingernail to push back each cuticle in turn, promising this would give me larger, more rounded fingernails.

Of course, there was a three-decade gap in her attentiveness when she disappeared into the hobbit hole. Yet after the death of Mr Phillipps, there were signs of interest. She collected my newspaper columns, occasionally telling me she liked them and often praising them to others, including the couple who ran the Noosa newsagency. When I reconstruct her attitude to me, the really negative years – the years in which she was hostile and dismissive – all coincided with Mr Phillipps. Maybe my father's version had at least some measure of truth: the story of a completely normal family disrupted by that bastard Phillipps.

Which is not a bad theory until you remember the alcoholic father, the fake-past mother and their virgin-birth child.

*

I wonder why I want to tell these terrible stories about my parents – their relatively moderate neglect; my father's relatively moderate alcoholism; my mother's unremarkable attempt to clamber up the social ladder. Even her sudden departure with a lover is, after all, the most unoriginal sin. Would I like it if, in twenty years time, my sons wrote a similar book about me – pointing out my failures; going through any documents I'd left; noting the nights I drank too much or told the same anecdote twice? How fair am I being? What right of reply do my parents have? Is it reasonable to blame my mother for sending me to Lionel in London? Don't I bear some responsibility for what happened? And if I'm going to mock my father for his problems, shouldn't I start with my own middle-aged self beset with the same issues? Drinking too much? Yes. And also a pretty good persecution complex: 'Why are those radio listeners texting in each day on the subject of my grammar, or my politics, or my speaking style? Why are they trying to *crucify* me?'

And then there's the additional complexity: is the point of these self-critical queries, so deftly inserted into the text, merely a plea for the reader to leap in to reassure the writer: 'Oh, no, everyone has been clearly beastly. You've been through so much, you poor dear ...'

Or – here's an alternative and sunnier theory – have I been blessed with a good story and decided to tell it, hoping it will chime with others? I want to believe there's a point to this tale – that so many of us have strange or neglectful families and yet somehow most of us survive. Here's what I hope is true: that these things happened and I want to make something of the story, turning it into an artefact that I can toss around in my hand, passing it to others to see if they find it useful. And then, more firmly than before, I can put it away on the shelf.

But first I need to know the full story. And that will take some research.

Chapter Thirteen

It was now a decade since I looked on the net and discovered the outline of my mother's family tree. It was also thirty-five years since my aunt first told me the real story of my mother's past. Why hadn't I been more curious? Why hadn't I tried to find my relatives? I felt some defiant pride in my lack of interest. Other parts of my life had gone well – my friends, my family, my career – and so I focused on these rather than on my parents. I had turned away from the parts of my life that were not nourishing and concentrated on the parts that were. I focused on the places in which I'd found love rather than on the places where love was missing.

When my younger son turned eighteen I wrote a piece for the newspaper listing all my best bits of advice for a young person – the things I wished I'd known when I was his age. In a long list, there was one idea to which people responded strongly:

Surround yourself with people who bring out your best side –
people in whose company you become fabulous, funny or wise.
Avoid people in whose company you become boring or sad.

Some readers told me they'd been inspired by that paragraph
to finally shake off that old 'friend' who'd spent decades making
them feel bad. Perhaps it was also good advice in terms of
parents: if they are awful, ignore them. I know this is contrary to
all professional counselling – 'You must resolve your issues with
your parents before they die' – but sometimes the parents you've
been allocated are unsuitable for that process.

And my quest to hold my parents at a distance had been
pretty successful. My weekly phone calls to my mother were
an act of duty, emotionally unengaging. I'd tell her about the
children and Debra, while understanding that her only real
interest was herself. Each week, before she was captured by
dementia, she'd talk about the late Mr Phillipps: 'You found him
for me,' she'd say at some point. By this time I would have heard
the phrase, or some variant, hundreds, maybe thousands, of
times. It was the 'Hello, how are you' of our every conversation.
The bit about Mr Phillipps would then lead on to my father
and his various defects, just as it had when we visited her in the
Enchanted Girdle. I would wait on the phone, sometimes lifting
it away from my ear so I could hear my mother's voice but not

her words. After some minutes the voice would stop, I'd return the phone to my ear, and say: 'So, have you been to dinner at the club?'

And yet, for all that I'd kept my distance, there was something intriguing about my mother's story.

I decided to buy a subscription to a genealogy website to see what more I could discover about her past. Ten years on, the site was more sophisticated than the one I'd visited in that burst of curiosity after my father's death. Within half an hour, I'd found several mentions of my mother's father, Harold Sudall – the one she always described as 'having worked for Sir Winston'.

A document came up showing that he had joined the army during World War I, enlisting on July 11 1917, giving a pub as his address: The Borough Arms, Cross Street, Accrington. I stared at the recruitment papers, his age (falsely) recorded in a looping script as eighteen years and six months, his trade given as 'motor driver and engineer'. There was something intoxicating about the image on my computer. With the website's help I worked backwards through Harold's life. I found him at age eleven in the 1911 census, one of a family of seven living at 18 Meadow Street, Accrington. Using Google Street View, I brought up an image of the house. It was still there: a squat two-storey terrace with a narrow door. It was a world away from my mother's tales about her aristocratic past.

Through the genealogy website, I tried to track down my mother's two older sisters. I couldn't find anything about the older one, Molly, but Bertha seemed to have married twice. One of the marriages had produced a son, possibly still alive. How odd it would be, after all this time, to meet someone from my mother's much-denied side of the family. Bertha's married name, I discovered, was Hartley-Smith. I typed it into a search engine and found multiple versions of her death notice. I felt a pang of regret. She had died just three years before. If only I had attempted this a little sooner, I would have had an auntie to meet.

The death notice described Bertha as 'a mother to Colin', 'a mother-in-law of Margaret' and 'a dearly loved grandma and great-grandma'. I'd only been at this for half an hour but my family was growing apace. I searched for my newly discovered cousin, Colin, using all my Google skills. Nothing worked, so I went back to the funeral notice, which was my only solid lead:

HARTLEY-SMITH – On 15th October 2010 peacefully in The Sands BERTHA aged 90 years. The much loved wife of the late Albert Hartley and the late Alan Smith.

It gave the name of the funeral company, the local minister and her nursing home. I emailed all three.

A few days later, there was a reply. It was from Margaret, my cousin's wife. It was my first contact with the family who, according to my mother, didn't exist.

Hello Richard

Well, life is full of surprises! … Nothing could have shocked me into silence as completely as the phone call I received from the office at The Sands this morning just as I was setting off for work. Anne, the girl in the office, was delighted that her detective work had produced results …

Margaret told me her husband, my cousin, was a little unwell but 'tickled pink' to hear from me. Her email ended:

Do hope to hear back from you. I know that Colin would like to know what happened to his Auntie. I never met her but know that Bertha was very distressed that they lost touch.

While looking into my mother's background, I also grew more curious about my own origins – the 'procedure' that apparently led to my existence and the gynaecologist who had performed it. My mother, when describing my miraculous conception, had always been keen to mention the name of the doctor: 'It was Professor Malcolm Coppleson,' she'd tell anyone who'd listen. He was, she'd make it clear, a *society* gynaecologist of some prestige. Could he still be alive? If I really were the first artificial insemination baby in the country, he might remember me.

I hunted around and found a phone number: right name, right sort of suburb for a retired medical man. After a couple of attempts, I found him at home, now aged in his nineties. His voice was firm and cultivated. I explained how my mother had always claimed I was created through artificial insemination, organised by him. Professor Coppleson listened and then asked the date of my birth. He seemed to be treading carefully. 'Memory is a strange thing; you have to travel back through it,' he said. 'I'd like to think about it, to see if I can be useful.' I paused to give him a chance to say something, perhaps to either confirm or laugh-off my mother's story. Nothing.

'So I should ring you next week?'

'Yes, why don't you do that.'

I made a note in my diary.

*

Meanwhile, I composed a reply to my cousin's wife, wondering how frank to be. Should I spell out what I knew? Or try to tread softly, teasing out more details without saying too much? Oh, bugger it, I'll be frank. Here's what I wrote:

When I first came to the UK – about thirty-five years ago, when I was nineteen – my mother wouldn't give me the names of my relatives. I think she had reinvented herself in Australia as posher than she really was (!) and that was why she didn't want me to make contact. It's a great thrill, though, to finally have a sense that there is this other side to my family.

The next morning I logged on and there was a friendly reply, revealing a flurry of relatives. Margaret and Colin had two sons, both with children of their own. Molly, the other sister, had given birth to two girls, one of whom was still alive.

Of course, my main questions were about my mother. Did she really leave school at fourteen? Was the family really banned from the wedding? Did they come anyway, as I'd been told, standing outside in the rain, throwing confetti? I wrote back hoping to start a conversation with Margaret's husband, my cousin.

*

I again rang Professor Coppleson, who'd now had time to reach into his memory. He recalled my mother, describing her as one of his favourite patients, but said he was uncertain whether he'd helped her with artificial insemination. All he could do, at this distance, was confirm that the treatment was in use at the time.

'I remember it all vividly, the wife there with her legs up, waiting, and then, in this little curtained-off area, the husband, the poor bastard, had to produce some sperm. I have a strong memory of the scene, but I don't remember if we tried it with your parents.'

At Professor Coppleson's suggestion, I rang one of his younger colleagues, Professor Robert Lyneham, an expert in infertility. The fifties were before Lyneham's time, but he was happy to guess at the method. It wouldn't have been the turkey-baster of popular legend, he said, more likely a syringe and a cannula. They probably performed the procedure twice, on Day 13 and Day 15 of the mother's cycle. The attempt at impregnation would not have occurred at the hospital, but in the gynaecologist's rooms – 'a private arrangement'. Assuming no complications other than an unwillingness to sleep with the father, the chances of becoming pregnant would be reasonably high.

Later, after checking the academic literature, Professor Lyneham sent me links to various articles. As early as the 1930s – according to a piece in a 1934 copy of *Scientific American* – one hundred and fifty babies a year were being born in the United States using artificial insemination, with either donor sperm or that of the husband. The practice, it seemed, went back a whole lot further than I'd imagined. The celebrated Scottish surgeon John Hunter was the first to claim success – impregnating a linen draper with her husband's sperm back in the 1780s.

My mother's claim of a virgin birth still looked possible, but not her claim that I was the first child in Australia to be produced by this method.

It was then I flicked open a more recent article by the American medical historian Kara Swanson, published in the *Chicago-Kent Law Review*. Swanson was not at all convinced by the *Scientific American* article, and its picture of early, widespread use of artificial insemination. According to Swanson, the week after *Scientific American* published its story in the mid-1930s, the New York Academy of Medicine tried to talk things down. It issued a statement declaring that artificial insemination was potentially dangerous, not very effective and certainly not mainstream medical practice. Even in the forties, artificial insemination, whether by husband or donor, remained a 'clandestine practice'.

To quote Professor Swanson:

The way doctors practiced artificial insemination, the strictures placed on patients, and patient access to the treatment were all shaped by fear of social opprobrium … the majority of doctors who practiced artificial insemination worked without any public admission of their participation in assisted conception, keeping their involvement quiet even as they urged secrecy on their patients.

By the 1940s the two variations of artificial insemination were often referred to as 'artificial insemination by husband' – or AIH – and 'artificial insemination by donor' – AID. The latter was highly controversial – 'adultery in a test tube', in the words of one Canadian judge – and even when it was the husband's sperm not everyone was happy. Again quoting Kara Swanson, it remained 'socially questionable and subject to religious condemnation'.

When the husband's sperm was used, the usual reason was to overcome fertility problems – either due to the 'barrenness' of the woman or a husband whose sperm was 'not vigorous'. The procedure, in the phrase of the time, would give the sperm 'a three-inch boost on a six-inch journey'. What about its use for women simply unwilling to copulate? Here the literature is silent. Perhaps the problem was simply too embarrassing to mention. I emailed Professor Swanson and asked her about my mother's situation.

She kindly replied a few days later:

By the 1950s, psychoanalysis was ascendant in the United States, and many doctors would have considered female frigidity to be a pathology that probably rendered a woman unfit for motherhood. On the other hand, providing a woman with a baby could also be a treatment for her disorder. I cannot comment on the extent to which such views would have prevailed in Australia at that time – in fact, I have not encountered any discussion of the practice of artificial insemination in Australia in the period that I have investigated.

The circumstances of my birth, while perhaps not unique, are still considered by experts like Swanson to be pretty bloody weird.

And maybe, just maybe, I was the first Australian case in this limited category: artificial insemination employed as a response to the mother's unwillingness to have sex. I rang Robert Lyneham to tell him what I'd discovered. He replied: 'I think a woman in those days would have to be quite brave to ask for it to be done.'

I imagined my father's humiliation, stuck in that tiny, curtained-off room. I thought about my mother, having to explain her situation. Maybe they did want me, to go through so much. Maybe I was a love child after all.

Top of the social pile ... my mother and father during
their early years in Papua New Guinea.

Chapter Fourteen

I was hoping to hear more from Colin, my newly discovered English cousin. While waiting I decided to assemble as much as I could of both my mother's and father's stories.

Father first: He was born on December 7, 1923, in Blackburn, a cotton town in the north of England. The address on his birth certificate was 38 Lynthorpe Road, Blackburn. He was educated at the Blackburn Cathedral School. His father was a foreman on the railways. My father first found work as an office helper at the *Blackburn Times*, a local weekly newspaper. He joined the Royal Navy in August 1942 and was seconded to the Free French Naval Forces as 'a liaison officer in sub-chasers'. At age twenty, he was promoted to sub-lieutenant, and then lieutenant by the end of the war. At some point he was selected to work on the *Pacific Post*, the newspaper of the British Pacific Fleet, published during the war's final months, becoming the paper's sports editor.

When the title ceased publication, he was appointed a press liaison officer with the navy's South East Asia Command, a role that took him to Hiroshima not long after the detonation of the nuclear bomb. In a box of his papers, I found a description of Hiroshima that he had written for his old newspaper in Blackburn, under the headline 'Blackburn Man Sees Hiroshima':

> My guide opened his face in a wide grin and spoke excitedly. His frost-bitten hand pointed out over the side of the balcony and he suddenly raised his hands skywards. I nodded my head to signify that I understood. It was not hard to gather what he was trying to tell me for we stood on the top floor of one of the half-dozen buildings that are the remains of atom-smashed Hiroshima.

Nestled with the clipping were three photos Ted took while in Hiroshima, marked on the back in his handwriting: 'Hiroshima, Japan, Feb 1946' – about six months after the bombing. The most dramatic shows just two buildings standing in an otherwise flattened plain. Among his papers were also two tiny metal Buddhas, wrapped in a cotton handkerchief. He told me he'd picked these up from the floor of a temple in Hiroshima and, later in life, suggested all his medical problems had been caused by the radiation they emitted. I never believed that claim, preferring to blame the countless whisky bottles, but nonetheless found myself pushing them to one side of my desk, using the end of a pen, so as to protect myself from any atomic radiation they might still be emitting.

He married my mother in late 1946, the scene captured in a clipping he'd kept from the local paper. The newspaper's photo showed him in uniform, my mother looking glamorous, her arm through his. The shot was close-cropped, just the two of them, so it was hard to know if, out of frame, there were the weeping relatives my aunt had described, throwing confetti in the rain.

As for my mother, the available facts were limited. Her birth certificate listed her as born on December 11, 1924 and gave her name as Alice Sudall. Her father's occupation was 'cotton mill engineer'. The address on her birth certificate was 46 Charles Street in Clayton-le-Moors, a town near the cotton industry hub of Accrington in Lancashire. This was about six kilometres from my father's family home.

Using Google's Street View I could bring up images of both addresses. I couldn't quite pick the exact houses, but the two streets looked almost identical. In class terms, my parents were closely matched, even in a country so conscious of tiny distinctions that George Orwell could famously describe himself as 'lower-upper-middle-class'.

I found my father's passport, showing the couple's arrival in Australia in 1946. In his box of papers, there were mentions of work as a sub-editor on Sydney newspapers – the *Sydney Morning Herald* and the *Daily Telegraph* – and then, in 1948, he was given the job of editing the *South Pacific Post*, a start-up English-language newspaper in Papua New Guinea, working under a managing director. He was twenty-five years old.

At the time, Papua New Guinea was a territory of Australia, with an Administrator running things from Port Moresby, assisted by Native Advisory Councils. When my parents arrived, there were – to use the wording of the time – around 10,500 'Europeans', 2500 'Asians' (a reference, largely, to the Chinese community) and about 1.5 million 'Natives'. The country's geography – chains of mountains as high as Europe's Alps, separated by deep enclosed valleys – created isolated, and sometimes warring, groups. In the 1950s around 850 languages were spoken. There were few roads outside the main centres and the coastal strip; transport into the Highlands was dependent on small planes operating from alarming makeshift runways. It was still common for expats, my father included, to have 'first contact' experiences, in which they would come across a village which had managed to avoid any interaction with Europeans. The *1954 Handbook of Papua and New Guinea*, a copy of which I found among my father's things, marks large parts of the Highlands as 'unexplored'.

The relationship between whites and locals was patriarchal. From the *Handbook*:

It can be said that these people, by and large, are likeable folk, developing a remarkable degree of intelligence when given reasonable opportunity; and that, other things being equal, a happy relationship can be established between Western Europeans and the primitive aborigines of Papua and New Guinea.

In the early 1950s, Port Moresby, the capital, had a limited phone service, only a few sealed roads and an exclusive club, the Papua Club, where European businessmen and public servants would meet. The *Handbook* of 1954 lists by name much of the European population, including Glover EP, Editor, of Kermadec Street.

The bus service in Moresby, according to historian Ian Stuart, was segregated. A section of the local beach was reserved as a 'European Swimming Beach', and part of the wage of any 'Native' had to be paid in the form of food rations. Papuans were employed in local shops but did not wait on European customers – they were there to fetch and carry under instruction. In 1956, the first milk bar opened: Papuans were served from one side of the counter and given paper cups while Europeans sat on the other, sipping from glasses.

It would have been a struggle to establish a newspaper. Newsprint was still rationed, printing machinery was difficult to source and the power supply was unreliable. Ships called about once every six weeks and a lone DC-3 aeroplane made a weekly trip between Papua New Guinea and Australia. Not only did my father have to find equipment under these constraints, he also had to hire staff. I remember him late in life telling me how he wandered down to the shoreline in Moresby and approached local men fishing off the rocks, offering them paid work as linotype operators – handling the hot, noisy machines which cast molten lead into lines of raised type. He smiled ruefully at the memory and considered whether their lives would have been happier had they refused his insistent offers.

It took months to produce the first edition, after which the paper limped through its initial two years, battling bankruptcy. The original managing director left, and my father became editor-cum-manager. A little later, Steve Stephens – the man who years later came to my rescue – was hired from Sydney to join the staff, adding a fiery tone to the paper's news columns. One historian of the period described him as 'an aggressive and outspoken reporter'. A decade on, the staff had grown to thirty-five Europeans and forty-five locals. Solvency had been achieved.

Years later, when Steve Stephens looked after me, he'd tell stories about those early years, describing the long hours working in the newspaper printing plant, a blazing-hot tin shed on the edge of Port Moresby. On one occasion, driven mad by the heat and noise, he had a furious row with my father, jumped into his car, drove the few miles to his house, ran up the front steps into his bedroom, opened the cupboard door, got his gun, loaded the thing and drove back to the printing room.

'It was only when I was walking through the door with the intention of shooting him that I thought, "Better not."'

Steve told me this story in the spirit of 'If I hadn't calmed down, you wouldn't have been born, so you owe me one there.'

*

An article from *Time* magazine, dated July 6, 1959, discovered among my father's papers, gives a good idea of the difficulties confronting the newspaper:

> Few more improbable newspaper locales could be conceived than New Guinea, 312,329 square miles of steaming, often impenetrable jungle and snow-capped mountains, populated by some 2,400,000 natives – 90 per cent illiterate – and some 34,000 émigré whites. Yet for nine years the Post has successfully managed to give a voice to an area where news once travelled largely by bush telegraph.

It went on to describe the *Post*'s 'termite-honeycombed headquarters', saying they'd been flooded eight times during monsoons. What's more, 'Twice the composing room has been invaded by serpents – a ten-foot python, a rare and venomous taipan – which were pelted to death by ingots of type metal.'

The author, *Time*'s Australian correspondent, described the paper as toughly critical of the island's Australian administration and noted the way the *Post* demanded justice for 'coloured readers'. He quoted my father: 'Nobody ever got hurt by free speech except bad politicians and complacent bureaucrats.'

I let the phrase roll around my head, admiring both its sentiments and its rhythm, feeling a surge of pride across the decades. The *Time* article is a tiny window on my father; it had been sitting in its box under my house for years without me knowing it was there. He'd kept six copies.

The piece also mentioned an unusual feature of the newspaper's success – some of the sales were to English-speaking expats, but others were to locals who used the paper to make roll-your-own cigarettes. This, six years on, led to a listing in the 1965 edition of the *Guinness Book of Records* under the heading 'Most Smoked Newspaper': 'New Guinea's *South Pacific Post*, which circulates only 5200 copies over about 183,500 square miles, is probably the most sought after newspaper for smoking and sells for 6d. per lb. for this purpose.'

Many journalists boast about their inflammatory prose, but my father's editorials were regularly proved combustible.

*

As I sat going through all this memorabilia, I felt a mix of delight and then misery for how it all played out. How could a life begin with such hope and intelligence and achievement and then end as it did? Whose fault was that? His? My mother's? That bastard Phillipps'?

I poured another glass of wine while I thought about it. And then another. Then another. I guess it's not hard for the grog to get a grip on a man.

*

I had the phone number of a woman in Melbourne who'd known my parents in Papua New Guinea, so I made a call. Her name was Heather Grey and she was about eighteen at the time I was born. Her father had owned the local brewery and her parents were once part of Port Moresby's European community. We made our introductions, with Heather hardly pausing for breath before setting forth a description of Moresby's expats, the words tumbling over each other, painting the social scene as insular, stratified and all white.

'Managers would mix with managers and clerks with clerks,' she said.

Heather remembered my mother as incredibly glamorous – 'the epitome of style' – always wearing gloves, a hat and stockings, despite what Heather called 'the stinking tropical heat'. She was already known as Bunty, having at some point discarded her given name, Alice. Heather also remembered my parents' house – an elegant building on a hillside. Taken to dinner there by her parents, Heather was told to wear her very best dress. Ted and Bunty, she said, were 'the top of the social pile; everyone wanted to be in their orbit'.

I mentioned that I was researching my family's history and confessed, 'I don't think my parents were as posh as they made out.'

'Well, good on them,' said Heather. 'In that case they had everyone fooled.'

*

I made email contact with another expat, Sue Voegeli-Sefton, who wrote back describing her life growing up on a rubber plantation at Koitaki, near Port Moresby:

> *Your parents were frequent guests at weekend house parties, which were at their stylish height around the mid–late fifties. Life at Koitaki followed the rhythms of the Raj. Everybody changed for dinner which was never served before 9pm. My sisters and I always gathered in your parents' room to watch Bunty change for dinner. We were in awe of her*

glamour as she sashayed around the room dressed in just a silk half-slip,
pretty bra and pearls around her neck. I must have been about eight years
old at the time and I can remember thinking she was like a movie star!

Sue's memories of my stylish mother chimed with the photos I'd found in my father's collection. Amid the images of indigenous warriors, bare-chested with elaborate headwear, there was a photograph of my mother being presented to Prince Philip, the Duke of Edinburgh. My father, his back to the camera, was standing rather stiffly to attention by her side. It was November 1956 and Philip was on a five-day visit to Papua New Guinea en route to the Olympic Games in Melbourne. My mother was wearing an evening gown with long white gloves. She had the Queen's husband hooked with a smile which he eagerly returned.

Like my father, she was all possibility; a young woman going places. This is the trouble with real-life story arcs: the happiness is so rarely saved for the end.

*

My parents returned to Sydney in 1961, after thirteen years in Port Moresby. Searching online, I found a clipping about them in the social column of the *Sydney Morning Herald* of October 29, 1961:

The Papua Club, 1956: my mother hooks Prince Philip with a smile.

LOVELIEST Harbour view in Sydney is that from Ted and Bunty Glover's sweet little gate house at Fernleigh Estate in Rose Bay. They took full advantage of it last night when they had twelve guests in to dinner in the courtyard.

By this point my father was managing director of Shipping Newspapers Ltd, a trade publisher, and my mother was on her way to joining the Sydney social scene. It was sixteen years since the end of the war and the girl who'd left school at fourteen had already met Prince Philip, wowed Port Moresby and was about to take on Sydney's eastern suburbs.

I found myself cheering her on.

From the clippings kept by her and my father, I reconstructed the story of her social ascent. First she won a place on the committee of the Metropolitan Opera Auditions – a group which raised money to help Australian opera singers travel to the United States to audition for the Met in New York. The group was laden with Sydney's elite, including Lady Mary Fairfax, wife of the patrician Sir Warwick Fairfax, owner of the *Sydney Morning Herald*. The committee staged large parties, normally at one of the Fairfax homes – either the one in the eastern suburbs, looking out to the harbour, or their country manor. A memory came back to me of trailing behind my mother as she marched down the multiple terraces of the eastern suburbs house in preparation for one of the parties. I also remember visiting the Fairfax country property, complete with a circular drive, grand steps going up to an open doorway and a butler standing in uniform. I'd never seen anything like it. I was probably seven or eight. I remember my mother excitedly telling me that the main bedroom had a button you could press and the roof would roll back so you could see the stars as you were lying in bed. Did she make this up or could it possibly be true?

The news clippings gave an overview of her progress:

Vogue Australia, 1962: She's photographed in a fancy hat, among a group of fancy-hatted women – 'members of a Rose Bay, Sydney, luncheon club: pretty young matrons having a pre-Christmas gathering'.

Sydney Morning Herald, Women's Section, March 7, 1963: There's a long article about the house my parents are building 'on the North Shore'. My mother's quoted: 'In winter we'll keep a stack of firewood in the storage room. Then it will only be a step – under cover – to get more wood for the library or the drawing-room fire.'

Sun-Herald, July 10, 1966: Mr and Mrs Edward Glover are photographed at a 'party to aid opera auditions held in a home in Vaucluse'.

Daily Telegraph, **June 13, 1969**: A profile piece marks my mother's appointment as 'promotions officer' with the Elizabethan Theatre Trust, handling both The Australian Opera and The Australian Ballet. "'I practically forced myself on them," said an attractive, fair-headed Mrs Glover.'

Daily Mirror, **June 19, 1969**: A fashion spread on her taste for knits. 'Bunty attributes the fact she can wear knits with no trace of bulge to yoga. "It's the greatest figure controller I know. When I get home from a hard day's work and have to give a dinner party for twenty-four or go out, just standing on my head and doing yoga breathing for a little while works wonders."'

By 1969, when this last piece appeared in the *Mirror*, I would have been ten years old and I can't say I remember walking in and seeing my mother standing on her head, but – who knows – maybe she did so in the privacy of her bedroom. Presumably she would run in at 6pm after work, thinking 'Oh my God, I've got to put on the canapés, but first I'll just get up on my head.'

*

While tracking my parents' life in Australia, my research continued into the family my mother had left behind. It was ten days since I'd first made contact with Margaret, Bertha's daughter-in-law and my conduit to my mother's secret family. First thing in the morning, I found an email from Margaret waiting for me:

> *Sadly, Richard, you contacted your long-lost relative just in time. Colin died suddenly this morning. I am naturally still in a state of shock but felt that you should know. We will no longer be able to pick his brains over family members, but hopefully I will be able to fill in a lot of the blanks for you. Please do keep in touch. M.*

It was just a coincidence, of course, this death that came so rapidly after I first made contact. But it felt creepy. For a second, I thought it was somehow my fault, as if I had brought the poison of my family life into theirs. It was a fleeting, superstitious notion, but one that fitted with thoughts I'd had before: the idea of my parents as a source of contagion. Once I'd managed to have my own family – when I found Debra, loved her, had children, knew it was good – I was sometimes overcome by fearful fantasies. I imagined my parents somehow reaching in and wrecking the life I'd managed to create. On the few occasions my family drove in my mother's car, I'd have a premonition that she would crash. Debra and I would be all right but one of the children would die. Or if my father slept over, maybe on the night before Christmas, he would get up drunkenly during the hours of darkness and accidentally start a fire. The fire would kill one of the children.

My parents could hardly be blamed for these mad thoughts: they were more about me than them. Perhaps I felt I didn't deserve the happiness that had come my way. Or that I'd had a lucky escape from my past and that somehow it would reach out and haul me back. And it's important to say my mother never crashed her car and injured my children; my father never started a fire. People are not responsible for the monstrous images you create of them, even if they are your parents.

I wrote back to Margaret, expressing my shock and sympathy. I also, at Margaret's urging, made contact with Molly's daughter, Dorothy – my other maternal cousin. I'd missed meeting one cousin by putting things off and now realised what a mistake that had been.

*

If there was a hole at the centre of my mother's story, it was Harold, her father. The genealogy site I was using had only the most basic information.

I tried a different site, with more of a British focus, and again typed in Harold's name. It threw up the documents I'd seen before – the census records for 1901 and 1911 – but also something new: an identity certificate from the merchant navy. I clicked on the file. Remarkably, it featured a photograph. I was seeing my grandfather for the first time. I was mesmerised. He looked like he was about nineteen, dressed in a jacket and tie, his hair slicked back. He had the same deep-set, widely spaced eyes as my mother. The document gave his profession as steward. Also included were his discharge papers from the merchant navy. They were marked 1923, when he would have been twenty-three years old.

Suddenly, after decades of prevarication, I was seized by a need to act. What had tipped me over? My mother's dementia? Seeing the photograph of my grandfather? Or understanding how I had already missed, by just a few years, the chance to meet my Aunt Bertha and, by a few weeks, the chance to correspond with my cousin Colin? Maybe it was all these things but, once formed, the urge was intense.

I needed to find out where I came from. And to discover what drove my mother to run from her childhood in such a dramatic way, brushing over her tracks and denying the existence of her sisters. It would require, of course, a trip to the place my mother had left nearly seventy years before.

I booked a pair of tickets to Britain with a plan to discover the truth.

The first photo I saw of my grandfather, Harold Sudall.

Chapter Fifteen

It was day three of our trip to the United Kingdom and I was cold and flustered. 'I can't quite remember his name,' I said to Debra. 'I know it's Nick, but is he the Earl of Cloncarty or the Earl of Clancurry?'

Debra stomped her feet against the cold. 'I'm pretty sure it's Cloncarty. He's the ninth earl or something.'

I checked my surroundings. There was the tower of Big Ben to one side. Westminster Abbey was behind me. And the Houses of Parliament were doing what they were meant to do, architecturally speaking: intimidating intruders. I strode towards a policeman, who was blowing on his hands to keep them warm.

'Is this the entry to the House of Lords?' I asked, adopting my mother's posh accent in the hope he would let me through.

'Are you meeting a peer, sir?' he asked.

Did I detect a tone of slight disbelief? With enormous delight I answered, 'Yes, actually, I am.'

My cousin Victoria – a relative on my father's side – had organised this trip to the House of Lords. I'd known her years before: firstly, when I visited Britain as a nineteen-year-old – she was the youngest of Auntie Audrey's daughters – then later when she spent four years in Australia working as a journalist.

I'd only recently discovered what happened to her once she'd finished her Sydney sojourn. After her return to England she'd married into the aristocracy. Yes, the aristocracy. Her husband was the Earl of Clancarty. Or to give him his full title: Nicholas Le Poer Trench, ninth Earl of Clancarty, and eighth Marquess of Heusden. He was a member of both the British and Dutch nobility. He had a seat in the House of Lords. He and Victoria had a nine-year-old daughter called Lady Rowena. Victoria herself, it emerged, was now a countess. If I were to properly address her, I'd have to say 'm'lady'. If only I could tell my mother: she'd spent a lifetime pretending to be an aristocrat. Had she stuck it out with my father, she could have been an actual aristocrat. Or to be more precise, she would have been married to a man whose niece was married to a man who had a seat in the House of Lords.

As for myself, I couldn't claim to be related by blood to the Earl of Clancarty, but I was certainly related by blood to his daughter, Lady Rowena. She was my third cousin, second cousin or vertical cousin once removed; I'm never sure of the terms. But we are pretty close! The important thing was that if 99.9 per cent of the British population were to die in a nuclear holocaust, I was now pretty much odds-on to become king.

*

Inside the Peers' Entrance of the House of Lords there was a reception desk, behind which stood a man wearing a white bow-tie and tails, with a large gold medallion around his neck.

'Who are you here to see?' he asked in a melodic Scottish accent.

'The Earl of Clarcorty,' I said.

'The Earl of Clancarty,' he said, smoothly correcting me, 'is expected soon.'

He asked my name, ticking it off on his list as another attendant scanned us with a metal detector.

'There are hooks for visitors where you can hang your things.'

Debra, still cold, seemed reluctant to give up her overcoat.

'Will it be warm inside?' she asked.

'Oh, yes,' said the Scotsman, winking, 'there's plenty of heating. It's taxpayer funded, you know.'

'Not my taxes,' said Debra, whose Australian accent was growing broader by the moment.

'Well,' said the Scotsman cheerfully, 'my taxes, then.'

We hung our coats and sat to wait. The attendants had

military bearing but a twinkle in the eye, as if this were somewhere between a court of law and a Butlin's holiday camp. At one point, an attendant passed us, leading a group of visitors. 'Walk this way,' he said, immediately adopting a comic gait, his arms flailing from side to side. Some lords wandered through, venerable old fellows, shuffling. A few minutes later, a youngish man with dreadlocks, decked out in an immaculate pinstripe jacket, appeared: Lord Groovy, I presume. Another minute on, we looked up to see a smiling, eager-faced man striding towards us, dressed in a suit but his hair a mess, like a nine-year-old boy pretending to be a businessman.

He reached out towards Debra, shaking her hand, then mine, exuding warmth and enthusiasm. 'I'm Nick. It's *so* good to see you.'

Moments later, Victoria arrived, also stomping her feet against the cold. She hugged us all; I remembered how fond I was of her and cursed myself for being so lazy about our relationship. She hung her coat on Nick's hook. The lobby felt like a primary school changing room – rows of hooks, each with a peer's name written underneath. Nick then led us through the back corridors, explaining the place as he went. In the past, all hereditary lords had the right to turn up and vote. Now, most of the members of the House were life peers – successful people nominated by the political parties for a period lasting their lifetime. In a compromise during the process of reform, ninety-two seats were allocated to the hereditary lords, with Nick elected by his fellow peers to fill one of them.

Victoria and Nick took us to the peers' dining room for lunch. There were white tablecloths and brisk, friendly waiters. One came up to take our order, inquiring of Victoria, 'And for you, m'lady?', and of Nick, 'M'lord?' Debra and I found this all quaint and strange, and Vicky and Nick seemed amused and appreciative, rather than jaded and born to rule.

By chance, the dining room had been in the headlines just a month before: a freedom of information request had revealed the most common complaints made by peers about the Lords restaurant. One lord had complained of a fifteen-minute wait to be seated which resulted in the loss of 'some of the finesse of the afternoon'; another said he had been left 'scarred' after his booking was cancelled suddenly. He complained that his wife had been 'unable to lunch elsewhere' because she was wearing a tiara. The lord recalled: 'We were only saved by the kindness of [a fellow peer] who offered us the use of his nearby home.'

Nick and Victoria – both tiara-free – offered us coffee, but then, checking his watch, Nick realised we had to rush. The afternoon session was about to begin and he was keen to hear the debate about the management of Britain's water supply. He hadn't yet decided how to vote. For someone like me, used to Australian politics, here was something new: a parliamentarian attending a debate in the hope of learning something.

*

While Nick's titles were numerous, the family's estates were long gone. Two days later we turned up at Vicky and Nick's home, a duplex in a town about ninety minutes by rail from London. The house was gloriously chaotic. Almost every room was lined with bookshelves which, despite their capacity, found themselves unequal to the task they'd been set. Giant teetering piles of books – art, history, literature – crowded each room, stacked beside chairs and covering every table top. A thin volume of poetry balanced atop a vase, no other place having been found for it. In the sitting room, you had to navigate your way from door to chair, stepping over books and stacks of artworks, many of them painted by Nick, propped against walls. Amid the lively mess ran Lady Rowena: eager, theatrical, smart. Nick and Victoria cheered on her various enthusiasms – her singing and her story-telling, and even her guinea pigs, any proximity to which sent Nick into an allergic meltdown.

Somehow Victoria coaxed a pot of tea from amid the stacks of books on her kitchen bench and we sat around the table late into the night talking about family and literature and politics, and admiring Nick's paintings which were vigorous, abstract and bold. I'd ignored family for so many decades. Who knew all this warmth and fun was on offer? How bad did I feel that Victoria had patiently waited for me to re-establish contact, to resume my role as her cousin? How foolish had I been?

*

The next day, Victoria cooked a bountiful lunch for the family. Her mother, Audrey, arrived, followed by Vic's sisters and then the sunshine. It was the first sunny day for weeks, as if even the British weather was conspiring to make me realise the joys of family. My two other cousins, Louise and Gabbi, were brilliant fun and we had an afternoon of sun-charged frivolity. None of this, though, was helping me with my quest to find out more about my mother. For that I needed Audrey and her memory. She was the only person I knew who'd been around when my father and mother met. I had so many questions. Had my mother developed her aristocratic claims before she met my father, or were they adopted to suit the stratified colonial scene of Port Moresby? Was there something about my grandmother and grandfather that explained why my mother turned her back on them? And what about the two sisters who'd been brought up with my mother, the self-proclaimed only child?

After lunch the two of us settled down at the kitchen table. I made tea, brought out my notebook and asked first about my father's side of the family. Audrey, my father's little sister, was in her eighties, graceful and smart, and eager to talk. She had a school teacher's urge to provide precise information.

'We were lower middle class. Your father went to Blackburn Cathedral School. That was a cut above elementary school, but a cut below a grammar school. Ted was always a go-getter. He met your mother right after the war. He'd just been demobbed and he met her on the train from London to Blackburn. He came home and said: "I've just met the woman I'm going to marry."'

'So you got to know my mother straight away?'

'Yes, I'd visit her quite often. She lived behind a bakery in Nelson in two rooms shared with her friend Peggy, Peggy's mum and Peggy's mum's boyfriend, Jim. There was no bathroom; when you wanted to wash you'd strip down and wash at the kitchen sink. It was quite basic.'

'And did my mother have a job?'

'She left school early, she would have been fourteen, and then she worked as an apprentice in a hairdresser's shop on Preston New Road at Blackburn.'

'Did you like her?'

'Yes, I liked her.'

According to Audrey, my mother and her friend Peggy would travel in the first-class carriage between London and home. Their aim was to meet military officers, who at the time were given first-class tickets.

'So that means she put on airs and graces right from the start?'

'She was like that when I first met her,' Audrey replied. 'I remember getting dressed to go out one night and we were taking turns using the iron. I complimented her on her ironing and she said: "Oh, the nuns taught me how to do that at the convent." It was a strange thing to say. There was no convent and no nuns. I knew that, and she knew that I knew, but she still said it.'

Audrey reported that my mother had already changed her name – from the Alice she'd grown up with to the jolly-hockey-sticks Bunty. Her Sudall surname had also changed. While others in the family introduced themselves as *Sudd*-el, the 'sudd' rhyming with 'dud', and the 'el' short and flat, my mother elongated the name until it became Sue-*dell*. So Alice *Sudd*-el became Bunty Sue-*dell*.

'Did my father understand that it was all an act?'

'Yes, but he went along with the story. He was obsessed with her. He also wanted to go up the social scale himself.'

'So the social climbing was a joint project?'

'Your father was besotted by her,' Audrey repeated after a moment. 'He was a very talented musician, did you know that?

He had a band and played trumpet, but also clarinet and cornet. Your mother thought that was all a bit common so it had to stop.'

As Audrey spoke, I remembered a scalloped note advertising 'A Grand Dance' in Blackburn that I'd found among my father's papers. I'd assumed it was kept as a romantic memory of meeting my mother; more likely, I realised, he'd kept it because his band had provided the entertainment. Another thought came: my son Joe had developed into a fine harmonica player, good enough to win occasional professional work. His ability had always been a mystery in a family in which I'd never been able to locate any musical skill; well, now I could. I was starting to see the appeal of this family history stuff.

'What about the wedding?'

'It was in Nelson. All the men had to wear their uniforms. That was your mother's idea. Your father had been demobbed so he had to get special permission to be in uniform. The guests who had military uniforms were invited to be part of the photographs, but not those without uniforms.'

She mentioned Frank, the third sibling in the family alongside my father and Audrey. 'Frank was in the merchant navy and was asked to stand aside. He wasn't happy about this, so when the photographer arrived from the local paper, he took it upon himself to make sure they had the names right. The bride's name, he told them, was "Alice", not "Bunty". He also pronounced the "Sudall" in the way it was normally said. Your mother would have hated it.'

Audrey allowed herself a smile at this. Frank would have enjoyed his small act of revenge.

So did my mother's family really stand in the rain throwing confetti? Here the story changed slightly from what I'd remembered Audrey telling me when I was nineteen.

'Molly didn't come, but her sister Bertha came and so did her mother. They hadn't been invited but they came anyway. They just sat up the back, the two of them, crying. We didn't talk to them because we didn't know who they were.'

Later, Audrey said, she invited the pair to her own wedding in an effort to make up.

Audrey pulled out an envelope of photographs from her handbag and placed the contents on the table. There was a photo of my parents' wedding, a photo of my father as a young navy lieutenant, looking fresh-faced and hopeful, and one of Frank in his merchant navy uniform. Looking at the photo reminded her of a story. Frank, while in the merchant navy, visited my parents in Sydney in the late 1940s. He planned to stay with them for a week or two, but they sent him packing after a couple of days.

'That seems a bit mean.'

'Well, Frank would have been deliberately winding them up. He would have been bunging it on, extra working class. It would have been "Ee, by gum" and "We only used to bathe once a week." He probably said it all in front of their friends, just to make a point, and that's why they sent him away.'

Over the years there'd been moments of contact between Audrey and my mother, but often they'd been problematic. She recalled sending a T-shirt for me to wear when I was six or seven years old, and my mother sending it back with a note, explaining it was too small. 'All Australian children have chests two inches bigger than those of English children,' was the way Audrey remembered my mother's note. My parents had also returned to England for a visit sometime in the early 1950s and behaved so pompously that the family rapidly tired of their company.

Audrey had told me plenty about my parents, but nothing about my mother's family background.

'So, what about her parents – Annie and Harold? What do you know about them?'

'Nothing really. Although there was a rumour, but only a rumour, that the father had been in prison, crime unknown. Whether that was true or not, I really don't know.'

*

I had already made an appointment to visit Nick Barratt at the National Archives in Kew. Nick had been an advisor on the TV show about family history *Who Do You Think You Are?*. I wanted to ask him about the idea of a fake past and how often he'd come across such a thing. He would also be able to tell me where to begin my search for Harold.

The Archives are contained in a huge steroidal building, built as if to resist nuclear attack, in suburban parkland west of London. Nick was in his mid-forties, donnish and handsome. He bought us both tea at the staff cafe. As we settled in, I explained about my mother and her 'aristocratic' past, her change of name and the denial of her sisters. I expected him to say, 'I hear that story all the time, especially from Canadians and Australians.' He didn't. Instead he crinkled his forehead.

'That's not so common,' he said. 'What's common is for people to "big-up" their background, but only a little. You see marriage certificates and people have written "manager" as their father's profession, or "independent means" when the truth was a bit more ordinary. But creating a totally different past ...'

I pushed him, perhaps not wanting my mother's oddity to be revealed as truly bizarre: 'But wasn't that the point of Australia or Canada, you could go there and be anything ...'

Nick paused and sampled his tea. 'Well,' he finally offered, 'I did help one family in which legend had it that the grandfather had received the Victoria Cross, but somehow the medal itself had been lost. The reality was that the fellow had been court-martialled for being drunk and disorderly.'

I feverishly took notes. This was a bit more like it.

'Anything else?'

Again a pause and another sip of tea.

'When we were doing *Who Do You Think You Are?*, the fourth series, there was a program with John Hurt, the actor, and he was convinced he was Irish. He'd been told that his great-grandmother was the illegitimate daughter of the Earl of Sligo. We checked it all out and there really was no Irish connection. We presented it to him on camera and he was quite upset. It changed his idea of who he was.'

So phew, at least my mother had some company. Although, to be fair, Hurt's imagined past was generations back. And he never claimed to be an aristocratic only child.

'Have you ever heard something like my mother's story?'

'Not really. To be honest, in my experience Australians are mostly proud that they came from nothing.'

Before I left the Archives, I headed upstairs and spent some time in the main reading room, feeding the name 'Harold Sudall' into various online forms. Whether due to my incompetence or a lack of documents, everything came up blank. That fitted what Nick had told me: only selected court records had been sent to the National Archives. If Harold had been a criminal, as my aunt had suggested, the proof would lie in the County Archives for Lancashire, held in the small city of Preston.

I was heading north anyway. I was about to meet the family I'd been told didn't exist. Who knew what a day or two in the records office would reveal?

Chapter Sixteen

Debra and I were in the north of England, on the way to visit my cousin, Dorothy – my closest living relative on my mother's side. Debra turned towards me from the passenger seat of the hire car.

'What are you feeling?'

'Well, nothing much. I haven't met her yet.'

'But you are about to meet her. This is the only person you have ever met on your mother's side of the family.'

'Other than my mother.'

'Yes, other than your mother.'

'I did actually meet my mother, you know ...'

'I have a fair understanding of that. My point is that, well, you must be feeling something ...'

We'd had versions of this discussion ever since we'd met. Debra often asked me to analyse my feelings towards my strange mother and my difficult father. I always replied with variations of:

'Well, I don't really feel anything much. I just want to be dutiful so no one can say I wasn't dutiful.'

And then she'd say: 'You act like your relationship with your mother is a job you have to get through – completing the task, doing it well, but not really caring about it. As if you are a worker in some business you're forced to cheerfully endure. There must be a deeper level of feeling. It's not possible that you don't feel more.'

Maybe Debra was right to prod me. For years, writing my newspaper column, I'd tried to kill off the stereotype of the unfeeling, insensitive Aussie male. The 'me' character in the columns was often foolish and annoying, but he was emotional and loving. That aspect of the 'me' character, I'm proud to claim, was drawn from life. Perhaps I'd inherited my father's gregarious spirit; maybe it was the heart-on-your-sleeve influence of Canberra Youth Theatre. For whatever reason, I am an emotional person, sentimental even. I cry freely. I am demonstrative.

Except for one thing. My parents. On that score I'm the Shut-down Australian Male Exhibit Number One. I bottle everything up; I'm unwilling to study my feelings; I'm uncomfortable when people – this means Debra – start prodding. My feelings about my parents had long before been placed in quarantine.

Debra's concern about this – her fear that it was doing me damage – was part of the reason she'd encouraged me to make this trip, wondering if it might crack something open. I was unsure about that ambition. Cracking things open can sometimes leave nothing but mess. I didn't want to be one of those people who wasted their existence focusing on, and thus giving power to, the worst people in their lives. I'd talked to plenty of others who were obsessed by their past – preoccupied with bad parents, with predators who'd sexually abused them, with so-called friends who'd made them feel worthless – so much so that they missed out on living their actual, available, and possibly useful lives. Part of me wanted to create a new aphorism: 'The *overly* examined life is not worth living.'

Then again – I had to admit this – Debra might have a point. Not understanding what happened to you is a different way of giving power to whoever it was, whatever it was, that hurt you. I also didn't want to become one of those people who die unhappy, alcoholic, drug-addicted, alone, his children hating him, never really understanding why he'd never been happy.

*

We were driving along the seafront of Lytham St Annes – a northern seaside resort close to Blackpool. There were some Victorian hotels of the Fawlty Towers type and a beach fringed with sand dunes. Inland from the seafront were streets lined with tidy bungalows. After a few turns, we pulled up at the address I'd been given and Debra leaned over, giving me a searching look.

'Take a moment.'

'Okay, I'll take a moment.'

For once, I did what Debra suggested and considered the strangeness of what was about to happen. Most people grow up with their cousins. Even if they live overseas, cards are sent and presents are swapped. I could have met this woman – the daughter of my mother's sister Molly – thirty-five years ago, when I first came to England. Except back then I didn't know she existed. How could she exist when I was – to use my mother's perpetual phrase – 'the only child of an only child'.

After a few moments, a fit-looking older man in a tie and jumper opened the front door and walked towards the car in greeting. Debra and I clambered out to meet him.

'I'm Stanley. Dorothy's husband. She is *so* excited.'

He directed me to park the car in the driveway. By the time I'd finished, Debra was inside, both hands being held by Dorothy. My cousin was beaming at Debra in the way you might beam at someone who'd just arrived from the national lottery office with a cheque for a million pounds. As I walked through the door, Dorothy's gaze shifted to me. She had piercing eyes which were damp with emotion. We embraced.

Tea was offered and served. After some joyful chatting, I asked Dorothy what she knew about my mother and her early life with her two sisters.

'The three girls didn't live with their parents. They mostly grew up living with their grandparents.'

'Why was that? What was the problem with their parents?'

'Their mother was Annie; she was a lovely woman, very kind, very caring and generous. You would have loved her. The grandparents were from her side of the family.'

'Yes, but why didn't the mother live with her own children?'

'Maybe Annie lived there too, at least sometimes. I don't think anyone ever explained that. I know Molly always used to say that she'd been to twelve different schools, so the children must have moved about.'

'What about the father? What about Harold?'

'We saw a lot of Annie, but not much of him.'

'Someone told me about a rumour he had a criminal record.'

'Not that I know of. But they didn't really talk about him much.'

*

Dorothy brought out two Christmas cards dating from the mid-1950s, both sent from New Guinea. The first was addressed to

Molly and written by my mother. It was quite formal in tone, wishing the family a happy Christmas. There was a friendlier one the next year, sent by my father. And then there was a photo of me in Port Moresby, aged three. The year would have been 1961, which seemed to mark the end of the contact between my mother and her family.

Around this time, Bertha, the middle sister, bought a seaside business in Morecambe called the Sunshine Hotel – giving employment, and accommodation, to both her older sister, Molly, and their mother, Annie. According to my cousin, Bertha was tough and ambitious – requiring maximum work from her sweet-natured mother and pliant older sister.

'And, over the years, did any of them ever mention my mother?'

'Oh, yes. Annie used to talk all the time about "our Alice" and the fact that she'd gone. She was heartbroken by it.'

'And Molly? Did she ever mention my mother?'

Dorothy paused and seemed to struggle with her emotions, then she talked about her mother's death, and how it was preceded by a period of dementia.

'I would go and visit her and she'd say, "Oh, you've just missed our Alice. You know how she likes to come and go."'

*

At the end of the afternoon, we hopped back into the car. As we drove off, Debra reached over and rubbed the back of my neck.

'That was amazing,' she said. 'They were such good people.'

'I really liked meeting them. Even if I still don't know why I'm doing this.'

'What's your fear?'

'That it will bring up lots of feelings I don't want to deal with.'

Debra didn't say anything to that, but she did rub my shoulders a little harder.

*

We drove to the hotel we'd booked for the night. It was part of a big function centre close to Clayton-le-Moors, the town on my mother's birth certificate. The car-park was full and there was a queue of people at reception. They all looked as if they were there for the same event: nearly all female, middle-aged, loud with strong northern accents, over-excited, super friendly, singing out to each other as they queued.

Others already booked in, wandered through, carrying super sized glasses of white wine – great buckets of the stuff which they eagerly downed while they walked. It was 6.30pm and the atmosphere was one chardonnay off a riot.

'What's going on?' I asked one of the guests.

'It's a party!' she said. 'We're the Daniel O'Donnell North West Association. You know Daniel?'

I confessed ignorance, which produced a pained look.

'You know. The singer. From Ireland.'

I shook my head in apology and asked: 'So, what sort of singer is he?'

'Oh, a fantastic singer.'

'I mean, what sort of music?'

'Oh, all sorts. Country. Love songs. Ballads. All sorts.'

She smiled, pleased to have banished a little of the world's Daniel O'Donnell-related ignorance.

After bundling our bags into the room, Debra and I headed into Clayton-le-Moors for a pub dinner. We both spotted fish pie on the menu, which we knew – after two weeks in the UK – would consist of tiny flakes of fish drowned in white sauce. It would be entirely stupid to order the same thing again, so we both said, 'Let's have the fish pie.'

This time around the amount of fish was so tiny I decided the chef was a devotee of homeopathy, bringing to the white sauce a mere memory of fish, whispering the word as he stirred – 'fish, fish' – or maybe just humming a few bars of 'I Do Like to be Beside the Seaside' as he flung a litre of béchamel into the microwave. The beer, though, was fantastic – a flat, warm brew, with a vague after-taste of dead rat. My enjoyment proved I must be still genetically English.

By the time we returned to the hotel, the concert was over and Daniel himself had taken up a position in the corner of the foyer, being photographed with fans. There was a queue which revellers were enthusiastically joining, each person giving Daniel a kiss just as the camera went click. The whole scene was one of great happiness. Back in our room I looked up the Daniel O'Donnell North West Association to discover Daniel had a considerable list of achievements – fourteen Top 20 albums in the UK and more than 3.5 million sales – so the incredulity which had greeted my ignorance was justified. The Association's manifesto closed with this line: 'He is also our friend, how lucky are we!!' I found that sentiment pleasingly cheerful and optimistic. The members of the fan club were seizing all available joy.

Somewhere below us the fans were still there, laughing, clutching each other, a bit pissed, but not really pissed, posing for picture after picture with the ever-patient Daniel.

There were lots of grim things about the north of England – things my mother did well to escape. She'd missed out, though, on this: these gutsy, loving people, so keen on having a good time.

*

My ambition the next day was to spend considerable time at the Lancashire Records Office. I felt guilty, though, about Debra. Our trip wasn't turning out to be much of a holiday. She'd spent the last five years working on what had turned out to be a hit TV show: she was the co-creator and head writer of the comedy-drama *Offspring*, which meant a constant shuttle between Sydney and Melbourne. She deserved a relaxing break. It seemed she wasn't going to get it.

We'd been in the north two days and had yet to see the sun. The weather varied between full-on rain and a sort of defeated mist. It was as if the whole place had been photographed in black and white. This part of Lancashire was also sliced and diced by motorways; to drive five minutes down the road, you needed to get on and off the M65 two or three times. I was becoming convinced the M65 consisted of concentric loops connected by further loops of the M65, meaning you never really got anywhere.

As you drove around in circles, you'd look over various hillsides, each of which featured a huddle of blackened terrace houses – the 'barracks of industry', as someone called them. Nothing seemed to have changed since the 1860s, except they'd demolished the factory around which the barracks had been built, leaving you wondering why there was suddenly a row of tightly packed houses clinging to an otherwise empty hillside. Who lived there now and how were they employed?

These were the leftovers of the Industrial Revolution – the stinking, noisy, smoky era described by Dickens, Ruskin and Engels: rows of hastily built tenements, two rooms upstairs, two downstairs, filled with families of seven or eight children, everyone over twelve years of age working in the mills. It was a world of steam-powered factories belching smoke; blackened buildings; overflowing sewers; deafening noise; the stench of ammonia and dye; tanneries and piggeries built between the houses; children enduring twelve-hour shifts. It was the horrors of this part of England – the 'dark Satanic mills' – that created the labour movement, socialism, even Marxism.

This was not the world into which my mother was born, but it's the world in which her grandparents lived. Today I was in search of their son: Harold, born in 1900, give or take. Would I find his name among the criminals whose records were kept at the Preston archives? I put the address into the GPS and we set off on the usual route through fog and driving rain, on and off the M65, sometimes heading north, sometimes south. Some months later, we came across Preston, a big town with an exhausted air. Hyphenated place names are so common in Britain – Stoke-on-Trent, Stratford-upon-Avon – I wondered if Preston should consider one: Preston-past-its-Prime.

After some poking around the back streets, we found the Lancashire Records Office – a modern slab of a building, strangely elevated on a series of concrete poles, as if the occupants were hoping it would take off. It seemed a relatively rational response to life in Preston.

Debra settled down in the lobby with a novel while I perched myself in the document room, flipping through random records, trying to spot any mention of my grandfather. First, I checked an archive of papers from the Burnley police department, including a Register of Charges, each page consisting of a single offence: 'That on this day, at so-and-so-time ...' It was a catalogue of human misery: beaten-up wives, fist fights outside pubs, people who'd broken into a shop at night to steal food – all recorded in a police officer's flowing script.

There was also a Book of Orders. I attempted to flip though quickly, trying to spot the name Sudall, but it was hard not to be snagged by other lives. 'I am the wife of the defendant,' one entry read. 'He smacked my face and ran me out. I never went back. He has been cruel to me on previous occasions.' The woman said she was willing to accept a pound a week from the man and custody of the child, a deal which the court endorsed. The grime of the time seemed to seep from the pages.

It was fascinating, but, an hour in, I'd found nothing. I asked the two librarians for their advice, telling them the story of my mother, her fake past and journey to Australia, and the rumour that my grandfather may have been a wrong 'un. Maybe I hadn't been clear about the dates, because one librarian asked, 'Do you think he was transported?'

I replied, 'I'm talking 1930s. I know you lot think we're all still convicts, but ...'

She smiled a little nervously, unsure of my tone, and her colleague stepped in to save the moment: 'Is it a relief when you take off the ball and chain? Does it chafe on your ankle?'

As usual in Lancashire a joke.

After a little more colonial banter, they suggested I consult the Calendar of Prisoners, in which the accused were listed alphabetically. The first to be sent up from the storeroom was for the Lancashire City Sessions Court, 1929. I flipped through, using the index at the start of the records for each day. I'd been at it about forty seconds when something caught my eye:

1. **Sudall,** Harold, 30, traveller.

Offence – on the 12th Feb., 1929, breaking and entering the dwelling-house of Romei Alberto with intent to steal therein.

Tried before Recorder, 4 April, 1929.

Verdict – Not guilty.

So this was it – the source of the rumour mentioned by my aunt – a charge, but one for which he'd been found not guilty. I copied the page and kept going. Maybe this brush with the law had taught

Harold a lesson. I was ploughing through the Calendar at speed, my eye darting to the spot on each page where, alphabetically, you'd expect to find a 'Sudall'. There was week after week of nothing and then his name grabbed my eye once more.

10. Sudall, Harold, 30, salesman

Previous conviction – Once fined for obstructing police.

Offence – Stealing on the 14th May, 1929, one handcart and other articles, the property of Beatrice Marion Shanks.

2nd charge – Receiving.

Tried before Recorder, 29 July, 1929.

Plea – Not guilty.

Verdict – Guilty of receiving stolen property.

Sentence – 9 months h.l. [hard labour].

It was a jail sentence, and a fairly long one.

I pushed through another pile of records with no result and found I'd run out of time, the library about to close. I'd have to return in a day or two. That night, back in the hotel, I searched the local newspaper archives, using the information from the court documents. Both Harold's cases had made the news. In the first – the one where he was found not guilty – the jury accepted his alibi that he was elsewhere, visiting a sick friend. In the second case, he'd taken off with a handcart loaded with shirts – 'to the value of £75' – which must have been quite a haul.

At the time of their father's conviction, Molly would have been twelve, Bertha ten, and my mother just four years old.

My mother, it seemed, had been running away from more than I'd thought.

Chapter Seventeen

The next day, I'd arranged to visit my other surviving relatives: Bertha's daughter-in-law, Margaret, and her two sons, Andrew and Lee. The death of Margaret's husband, my cousin Colin, had only happened about six months before. I was worried about intruding on her grief, but her email expressed enthusiasm for our visit.

As we drove towards Margaret's house, Debra posed a question: 'When are you going to tell her about Harold and the one-man crime-wave that was your grandfather?'

'She might already know.'

'Bet she doesn't. Your other cousin didn't.'

'Well, I'm not going to blurt it out as soon as I get in the door. Guess what? The grandfather of your children was a thief. There's petty-criminal blood in our veins.'

'But you should tell her what you've found.'

'Yes, but I think I'll wait until the second pot of tea.'

Again the GPS took us to a tidy bungalow in a seaside town – in this case, Morecambe, the town where my aunt Bertha had owned her business, the Sunshine Hotel. Margaret's two sons were outside when we drove up: both in their late thirties, friendly and good-looking. They ushered us inside, where Margaret greeted Debra and me with hugs and delighted exclamations of 'Finally!' and 'I've been looking forward to this,' before showing us into the living room. Already, Margaret had some photographs splayed out on the coffee table and some stories to tell.

She started on a quick climb of the family tree, while I wondered when to introduce the topic of Harold and my fresh discovery of his criminal past. My restraint lasted about a minute and a half.

'Did you know that Harold was in prison? I've just been to the Archives …'

I offered the photocopies I'd taken the day before. Margaret picked them up and studied them with interest. Her two sons read over her shoulder and then Margaret handed back the photocopies with a shrug.

'I didn't know any of this.'

'So Bertha never mentioned that her father had done time?'

'That's not really surprising. If her father had been sent down it would have made Bertha clam up like an oyster. She was very cut-above and plum-in-the-mouth.'

'So she pretended to be posh, just like my mum?'

'Well, she was quite grand,' said Margaret.

Lee, the older son, laughed. 'Grand? Bertha was a real Hyacinth Bouquet,' he said – a reference to *Keeping Up Appearances*, the sit-com about a woman who pretends to be posh.

'She had one voice for the family and then another for people she wanted to impress. I'd come in and she'd say, "'Ello" to me, common as muck, then maybe I'd have a girlfriend walking in just behind, someone unexpected, and it'd be, "Oh, helloooo," then lots of "rath-er".'

Lee and his brother laughed as if they found the scene more ridiculous than objectionable. Lee was a great story-teller and performed a few more scenes pretending to be his grandmother, alternating between a Lancashire burr and a Hyacinth Bouquet bray.

And how did Bertha behave towards my cousin Colin, her only child?

'He was never treated properly,' Margaret said. 'When it was high season in the hotel, she'd just rent out his bedroom. She had this piece of plywood made up that would fit over the bath, and she'd make him sleep there – on top of the bath. He always said he had to spit in his own dinner otherwise Bertha would wrestle it from his hands and send it off to a paying customer.'

Lee and Andrew were both looking at their mum, shaking

their heads, imagining all that their dad had been through.
Suddenly we were on the verge of re-enacting Monty Python.

'Have I told you chaps about my mother and her lackadaisical
attitude to parenting?' I could have said.

'"Lackadaisical attitude to parenting?"' they could have
replied. 'Thy be lucky. Our father Colin had to sleep on t'bath
and spit in t'plate of own food.'

I could have added a new game to add to my set, this one
called Whose Parent Had the Worst of It?. Instead, we sat talking
about Harold, his time in prison and how it might have changed
his own children and his children's children. And then we all went
out for lunch.

*

Driving back to our hotel afterwards, Debra tried to put together
the picture so far.

'Of the three sisters, Molly seems like the sweet-natured,
compliant one. That's the case, too, with your grandmother,
Annie. Then you have this other personality type – Bertha and
your mother.'

'Exactly,' I agreed, 'a kind of self-centred fierceness. They
were going to look after themselves and climb out of whatever
hole they were in.'

'Your mother took it further, though.'

'Yes, Bertha pretended to be posh. But she still saw her mother and she still saw her sister.'

'Your mother's response was more dramatic.'

'Yes, but she was also the youngest. Maybe the older ones had more of a normal start before Harold turned to crime, and the children started shifting house all the time.'

For a while we drove along in silence.

Then from Debra: 'Reconstructing family history is like looking at a fossil and trying to picture the whole animal. You have the foot or the jawbone, then have to infer the rest from the fragment you've found.'

I agreed with that. I would never be able to properly summon up my mother's early life, but it still seemed worthwhile to ask the obvious questions. Was it really necessary for my mother to deny her past so thoroughly, right down to the existence of her own siblings? After all, in denying them, she had also denied their progeny – these people I'd just met, people who were not only warm and friendly, but smart and manifestly successful.

If my mother thought the only way to make something of yourself was to leave, then those who'd stayed had proved her wrong.

*

The next day I headed back to the records office, leaving Debra to visit Accrington's sole tourist attraction, the Haworth Gallery, which, she later told me, was closed for the day. From her point of view, the holiday was definitely falling short of a week in Paris. Back in Preston, I ordered another pile of documents. The fourth volume I searched was the County Borough of Blackburn Quarter Sessions Calendar 1931–1935 and there he was, yet again.

4. Sudall, Harold, 34, salesman

Offence – on 10 May 1933 obtained by false pretences 14 rolls of felt from Mercer and Sons Inc.

Plea – Not guilty.

Verdict – Guilty.

Sentence – 6 months h.l.

It was again a fairly lengthy sentence. My grandfather stood convicted of 'false pretences after a previous conviction of felony'. The order was given: 'that the above named convict be imprisoned and kept to Hard Labour in His Majesty's prison at Liverpool for the term of six calendar months, commencing on the said ninth day of October, one thousand nine hundred and thirty three.'

An hour later I found another passing reference. This time it was in a Register of Persons sent to Gaol. It was a handwritten list with not much detail, just the name Harold Sudall and the annotation 'breaking and entering; stealing money'. The document told me the name of the police officer who was to 'convey the prisoner': it was a PC Coupe. Somehow the name conjured up the scene – PC Coupe at the wheel of a 1933 van with Harold handcuffed in the back, on a round-trip from Liverpool Prison back to Liverpool Prison.

A few volumes more and I had another strike. This time it was eight charges of false pretences. He was found guilty on one of them: obtaining one pound, five shillings and sixpence 'under false pretences from Laura Cousins'.

The document listed his prior convictions, which were becoming numerous:

- 9 months hard labour, Manchester City Quarter Sessions, 1929, receiving.
- 3 months hard labour, Preston Sessions, 1932, larceny, after previous conviction for felony.
- 6 months hard labour, Blackburn Borough Quarter Sessions, 9 October 1933, false pretences, after previous conviction of felony.
- 9 months hard labour concurrent from 10 October 1933, Burnley Borough Quarter Sessions for false pretences.
- Also seven convictions for gaming, drunkenness etc.

I did some quick arithmetic, taking account of jail sentences that were served concurrently. From mid-1929 to mid-1934, Harold had clocked up two years in prison. From my mother's fifth birthday until her tenth, her father was in jail a little under half of the time.

His criminal ubiquity was such that I came across another document within another half-hour. There was one fresh crime added to the previous litany: a charge of 'attempted larceny by trick'. Later I found a newspaper report that described the crime under the headline: 'Gilded Coin Trick'.

The article, in the *Manchester Guardian*, recounted how my grandfather had asked to borrow two pounds from a Blackpool confectioner called Ruth Holt. He offered as security a gold coin, which he said was a two-pound piece, 'but which was actually a gilded coin'. The case made no sense. I suddenly wished I had been a lawyer, arguing in my grandfather's corner. Why would anyone want two pounds in return for two pounds? Why would Ruth Holt give him two pounds in return for two pounds? Why wouldn't she just say, 'Mate, you've already got two pounds'?

According to the newspaper article, my grandfather blamed the whole thing on his employer, a steeplejack called George Freer. My grandfather's argument was that Mr Freer's car had broken down and Mr Freer had given him what turned out to be a fake gold coin with the instruction to swap it for a real one so that he could repair his stranded vehicle.

Harold's alibi seemed vaguely plausible until the police prosecutor jumped up to ask Mr Freer a question about his broken-down car.

Police prosecutor to George Freer: 'Do you have a car?'
George Freer: 'No. I don't have a car.'

Whatever the nature of my grandfather's criminal genius, coming up with an alibi wasn't always his greatest knack. He ended the day being sentenced to another three months in prison.

*

I found one final document: the date was 1936 and this time my grandfather was charged alongside an associate, William Harrison, forty-five, a labourer. The pair were charged with Breaking and Entering with Intent to Steal from the shop of Herbert Hardacre of Burnley. Both were found guilty, and this time Harold's sentence was lengthy: '15 months in the second division'. He was carted off again to Liverpool Prison.

That night I did a final calculation. On the basis of what I'd discovered, my grandfather spent at least thirty-nine months – three years, three months – in prison, for a total of eight crimes. He had also clocked up another seven summary convictions for matters such as gambling and drunkenness, and been charged without conviction on another handful of occasions. Later, I tried to use this information to find out more, but Harold seemed to disappear from the records. The final fifteen months in Liverpool Prison had, perhaps, shocked him into honesty.

For the years following his release, there was not much to go on. My cousin Dorothy had given me a photo of Harold and Annie sitting on a beach; he appeared to be in his late forties, respectably attired. I also found, via a genealogy site, a record of his will. Probate had been granted on his estate in October 1951, which means he died when he was just fifty-one years old. By that time he was living at 2 Westhall Road in Bath, another tiny terrace. He didn't leave the world with much: 176 pounds and sixteen shillings. It was left to 'Annie Sudall, widow'.

Some months later, Margaret sent me a copy of Harold's death certificate, which she had located among Colin's papers. It listed the cause of death as coronary thrombosis and arteriosclerosis and gave his occupation as 'Supervisor/overseer at the Admiralty'. So maybe he did go straight for the last thirteen or fourteen years of his life. And, in the end, he did 'work for Sir Winston'; well, sort of. The death certificate informant was Annie, and her address was 2 Cedar Grove, Morecambe – Bertha's address – so my mother's parents were in contact, but living at different ends of the country.

I wonder if my mother even knew about her father's early demise. The last Christmas card to Molly had been in 1953, so I presume she was told. By 1981 when Annie died, my mother was secure in the hobbit hole. All contact had been abandoned many years before. My guess is that she never heard of her mother's death.

*

We had one day left in the UK before catching the plane home. As well as documenting my grandfather's criminal past, I wanted a better sense of the place my mother had fled. Debra and I set out with a list of addresses, starting with the terrace house on my mother's birth certificate: 46 Charles Street, Clayton-le-Moors. It was two storeys, with a slate roof and a bay window, but squat and narrow. If you put two beds end-to-end, they'd be wider than the house. I took out my phone to line up a photo. A woman, probably in her sixties, was walking her dog in the park opposite and sang out as I clicked: 'Did it smile for the camera?'

A funny line as usual.

We wandered over and started chatting. She asked if we were considering buying in the area, so we told her about my mother and my quest. The woman – Diana – had a cheerful manner, although everything she said was sharply negative.

'Your mother was right to get out, you know. There are no jobs here now. Blackburn is the worst, but everywhere here is pretty bad.'

She pointed down the street to what was once the entrance to the English Electric Company, a heavy engineering firm.

'After the war, four thousand men used to work there; there'd be buses lined up and down this street to take them home. Now there's no work anywhere. It's a sad time in the north.'

'Is it really that bad?' I asked.

'My son is an accountant, he's overseas, working. And I said to him, "Son, do people still talk about Britain?" and he said, "No, Mum, they never do. The government thinks they are in charge of this big thing called Britain, but it's nothing. No one's ever heard of it."'

'Oh, I think that's an exaggeration,' I said, smiling, trying to cheer her up. 'I've heard of Britain. We've even come to visit it.'

'Well, maybe you have, but nobody else has even heard of it.'

Despite Diana's view that the UK virtually didn't exist – 'United Kingdom? Are you sure? You're not thinking of the United States?' – I decided to ask her about some local history.

'I read somewhere that Clayton-le-Moors used to be divided in two, along class lines – a bottom end and a top end. It said the two ends would hardly ever mix, but then, once a year, both sides would play each other in a game of soccer.'

Diana nodded, as if everyone knew this.

'So which end is this?'

'Oh, this is the bottom end.'

The dividing line – I knew from my reading – ran through the splendidly named Load O'Mischief Hotel.

'Is the Load O'Mischief still here?' I asked Diana.

'No, it was demolished in the 1980s.'

'Why?'

'To make way for the M65.'

Of course. Around here, the M65 is the answer to any question you may have the desire to ask.

*

I loved the combination of wit and misery that was always served up in the north; the dry humour doing daily struggle with the wet rain and the grey skies. On a previous trip to England, I'd had trouble finding my hotel in Liverpool. Chatting with the receptionist, I'd blamed the female voice on my GPS.

'She didn't know the name of your street,' I said. 'I'm going to have to throw her out.'

'Don't do that,' the receptionist replied, deadpan. 'Give her a chance to win back your trust.'

On the same trip to Liverpool, I asked directions of two paramedics, parked in their ambulance. One hopped out of the vehicle to show me the way, so I apologised for taking them away from their duties.

'Don't worry,' she said, 'we're just sitting here waiting for someone to die.'

Or – this is weird: again Liverpool, same trip – I overheard two mates in a pub, one teasing the other for being 'a wrinkly old bastard'.

First man: 'Those are just laugh lines.'

His friend: 'Mate, nothing's that funny.'

*

In Blackburn, a few kilometres from Clayton-le-Moors, I took a photo of the house in which my father grew up. Despite my Aunt Audrey's view that her side of the family was a tiny cut above my mother's, to my eyes the house was identical to all the others I'd seen: two-up, two-down, lane out the back. It was the same when we swung into Oswald Street, where Harold was born. Number 50, his parents' house, was part of a row of terraces, backing onto a cobblestoned laneway. It all looked like the Monty Python scene where they sing 'Every Sperm is Sacred'. Again, I took some photos. As I snapped, a man trudged up the hill with two shopping bags. His name, it emerged, was John, and he'd lived in a house over the road 'since I came here'.

'Where did you come from?' I asked, thinking this might be a story of immigration.

'Out of me mam. That's where I came from. In 1946.'

Again, funny.

Like Diana, he was not a big fan of the area, despite spending his life here. 'They don't need any people because there are no jobs.' He talked about his various occupations – working as a lathe operator at a local firm, then at Rolls-Royce, then at a factory where he screwed together sporting trophies: 'A cushy job, that one. I was sat down all day.'

It was just before noon and he told us that he'd just purchased five pints of beer from the shops: that's what was nestling in the plastic bags he was carrying. Inside his terrace, he'd already put his lunch into the oven. He described, with some pride, what he called his 'routine':

'I like to drink my beer first – and then eat. I eat like a horse because the beer gives you an appetite. And I've got five pints ready to drink now, right? So I'll drink them. My dinner is in the oven, cooking, so by the time I've finished the five pints I just eat my meal. I don't bother with television – I can't stand it. I go straight to bed and it's morning again before I know it. I sleep for ten hours right through, nobody bothers me.'

He seemed willing to offer his system – free of charge – to anyone else who might spot its considerable virtues.

*

We trudged around the streets. I felt a bit daft, to use a northern word, but I was looking for signs of my mother. I was trying to summon up an imagined childhood for her – to see her in these streets, walking home from school or playing with friends. She was proving elusive: I had this handful of facts at which I kept staring, broken shards in which I might see a tiny, fractured reflection of her. She was just short of three years old when her father was first sent to prison; by the time she was twelve, he would have been locked up for over a quarter of her life. In every court document he was listed at a different address. I'd been told my mother and her sisters lived with their maternal grandparents, the Boothmans, at their long-time home. But there was also Molly's recollection of having attended a dozen different schools. Now, with the assistance of the court documents, I could guess the pattern: when their father was out of prison, the three girls and Annie would shift between a series of tiny boltholes in Burnley and Manchester; then, when he was sent back to jail, it would be back to Annie's parents in Accrington.

I wrote out all the addresses I had for Harold, drawn from various documents. Starting when he was fifteen and living with his family at the local pub, the Borough Arms Hotel, until he was sent for his final long prison stint at the age of thirty-six, there were at least seven different abodes, not including the two places he just couldn't help returning to: Manchester and Liverpool Prisons. No wonder, when I went through my mother's things, she was lacking the sort of childhood memorabilia most people have, the sort of things I found in my father's flat – the illustrated school projects on 'Grand Houses of England'; the sports certificates and ribbons; the exercise book for junior arithmetic. I'd assumed she'd rid herself of this material in order to bury the evidence of a normal working-class childhood. More likely, she never had any of these things in the first place; the minutiae of her childhood had been lost as she shuttled back and forth between her grandparents' house and her father's various lodgings.

*

We walked and we drove. I was still feeling bad about Debra and her rather dreary holiday. I tried to apologise by making up the sort of headlines that might feature in a pamphlet describing our visit up north.

'Experience Genuine Lancastrian Fog!'

'Drive Up and Down the M65 Almost Constantly.'

'See Buildings Black with Soot!'

Soon Debra joined in and we merrily laughed our way down the M65.

Debra: 'Enjoy Fish Pies with No Fish!'

Me: 'Kiss Visiting Irish Singers!'

Debra: 'Discover your Grandfather's Criminal Past in Our
   Attractive Archives!'

Me: 'Drink Beer that Tastes like Dead Rat!'

Debra: 'Watch Husband Take Photos of Innumerable
   Doorways!'

Despite the weather and the M65, Debra warmed to the task, working up a routine about my family's criminal past.

'Ah, there's the courthouse,' she said as we drove through Accrington, 'a place that owes its imposing size to the existence of the Sudall family.'

Or as we passed the police station: 'I wonder if they've installed a blue plaque mentioning the Sudall contribution?'

Or pausing for a cup of tea in a cafe: 'I see they trust you with a silver spoon. Do they realise the Sudall gang is back in town?'

The two of us wandered out of the cafe and I promised that the afternoon would be more fun, at which point the fog instantly deepened, as if the weather itself was saying, 'You are still in Lancashire.' Everything felt slightly worn out. Most of the people on the streets were elderly; presumably anyone fleet of foot had fled. At the Oswaldtwistle shops – which you approach by simultaneously driving both ways along the M65 – they had a whole car-park reserved for disabled drivers. A smaller car-park over the road had been established for the able-bodied minority. In Clayton-le-Moors, the main street offered a corner store for rent: 'Ideal for hair, beauty, nails' said the sign, '£59 a week'. Rents this low were hardly the mark of a booming high street. My only question: since the factories all closed in 1967, why was everything still soot-covered? It was like being sweaty from some jogging you did when you were seventeen.

At the Oswaldtwistle shops, I bought a local paper, the headline of which claimed children in Blackburn were the most underweight in Britain: up to four hundred primary school pupils in the borough were suffering from malnutrition due to parental poverty. Later I found online a report into longevity commissioned by an advocacy group called Public Health England: several boroughs in this part of the north-west featured in the 'top ten' lists for the lowest life expectancy in England. In the Little Carleton area near Blackpool, boys born around now would likely live to the age of 67.3, a life expectancy worse than that in North Korea, where it's 69, and a long way short of Knightsbridge, the highest in England, where a boy born now will live until he's 97.7. In my father's home town of Blackburn, life expectancy for males was still rated as 3.2 years shorter than the English average.

The only places going gangbusters were the local supermarkets, which were stuffed with the world's produce. At the end of an afternoon of driving, we pulled into the capacious car-park of the local Lidl outlet. Our plan was to buy dinner and smuggle it back to our hotel, now eerily quiet since the departure of the Daniel O'Donnell fan club. We wandered aisles stacked with the best – well, the cheapest – the European Community could offer: Romanian pâté, German sausage and Lithuanian cheese. We assembled an enormously cheap feast. I added a £3.90 Chilean merlot to provide some cheer against the landscape. As we headed to the register to pay, I overheard a conversation between two middle-aged northern men, both pushing shopping trolleys.

'How's your boy doing?'

'Good. He's in remission.'

'That's great news.'

'Well, I gave him my stem cells. We're a genetic match, an exact genetic match.'

The father emphasised the word 'exact', and then smiled broadly, as if to say, 'Isn't the world a marvellous place?'

I pushed my trolley past, leaving them smiling at each other.

Chapter Eighteen

My mother was starting to come into focus; somehow her lies seemed less strange, less destructive. I saw her determination, her self-belief. How else do you cut yourself free from a difficult family unless through some quite brutal knife-work? The British class system is a terrible thing; it is pernicious and unfair. Maybe there was something admirable about a woman who refused to bow down to it; a woman who said: 'I'll just pretend to be something different and go to the other side of the world where no one will know the truth. Stuff 'em.'

Yet I'm still stuck with the old questions: did she have to also reject her mother and sisters? Make up a past? Talk endlessly about lavatories? Use that ridiculous voice? Behave in such a snobby way to other working-class people? Wouldn't a move to Australia have been enough? Wouldn't it have been more impressive to say: 'I came from this messed-up past then made something of myself'?

Thinking about all she went through, I find myself in a

forgiving mood – contemplating that tiny four-year-old whose father was marched off to prison. Then, a second later, I wonder if her brutal knife-work left her unable to form proper relationships with others. Among them, me. Should I think of her as someone who had the gumption to save herself ... or as just another shyster conning people in the colonies?

She wouldn't, after all, be the first person to travel from the UK to Australia and seize the opportunity to shake off her social class. Australian history has recorded similar deceptions. Arthur Orton, a butcher's son from London, came to Australia in the mid-1800s and claimed to be the missing heir to the Tichborne baronetcy – a fraud so brazen he managed to convince the real Tichborne's mother, who gave him an allowance of £1000 a year.

Or, closer to my mother's time, there was the Australian designer Florence Broadhurst. She was born poor in outback Queensland, travelled to Shanghai and London, where she pretended to be French, and then came back to Australia in 1949. Once here, she pretended to be an aristocratic English artist visiting the colonies in order to recuperate from the ravages of the war. She fooled most of the people most of the time, rising rapidly in Sydney social circles during the same period as my mother. Broadhurst created a business designing and manufacturing wallpapers for the homes of the well-to-do, and by the mid-sixties was well ensconced in Sydney's top drawer.

The Broadhurst story shows how easy it was at the time to adopt an accent and an attitude and to be taken for the real thing. Or, to put it another way, how the well-heeled of Sydney were hungry for the opportunity to rub shoulders with what they imagined were British toffs. I wondered if Broadhurst and my mother ever met – two women using identical methods to achieve identical results at pretty much the same time. I wondered, too, if either would have twigged to the other's bunged-on accent.

'Lavatory, Florence?'

'Oh, yes, Bunty, it's just through the drawing room. Do leave your napkin on the sofa.'

Broadhurst, as it happened, died a horrible death – brutally murdered in her studio. Some say her fake past was a magnet for her killer, who may have told similar lies. So, I suppose, there are ups and downs to this business of having a fake past.

On the other hand, the chance to break with the past is central to the Australian story – or at least to that part of the Australian story that doesn't deal with indigenous Australians and the theft of their land. Our modern history begins in 1788 with the dumping of the human detritus of Britain: people who were poor, mostly ill-educated, criminal. Yet, repositioned in the sunlight, they flourished. Given a similar experiment today, plenty of people would mutter about 'bad genes' and say, 'Well, that idea will never work.' And yet it did. This was colonial Australia's great gift to the world: practical proof that, when it comes to human society, the soil is more important than the seed. Maybe my mother was just an extreme, confabulating version of one of the world's most inspiring tales: how a country called Australia, full of air and sunlight, transformed the lives of the millions who took the chance it offered.

*

Back home, I recruited the help of a wise friend, Neil Phillips, who works as a psychiatrist, mostly helping people in pretty tough situations. We'd found a spare day in both our diaries – Anzac Day – and I headed to his house. He made us coffee, took a seat in an armchair and motioned me towards the couch.

Jokingly, I asked, 'Should I lie down?'

Jokingly, he replied, 'Well, you are here to talk about your relationship with your mother.'

Neil is New York trained, which in his case means the Freudian tradition; his Viennese mother had even attended lectures by the master. For all that, Neil tends to embrace the practical and the compassionate, rather than the five-days-a-week couch-fest of psychoanalysis. I remained sitting upright and we both chomped on Anzac biscuits. Between mouthfuls I told him, briefly, my mother's story and explained how I had discovered the truth when I was nineteen.

Neil has the ability to pose the perfect question. He asked, 'Did it trouble you when you found out?'

I answered honestly: 'Not at all.' I explained that even though my mother had often told me the story of her aristocratic background, I'd never paid attention to it. 'I was,' I added, 'pretty uninterested in my parents from an early age.'

If this was a film the music would swell up and the analyst would take an extra-long drag on his cigar. Instead, Neil just sat there and then said something so bleedingly obvious that naturally I'd never thought of it.

'I wonder if you were uninterested in your mother's story because it felt like it was made up. There was a superficiality there that you picked up on.'

He was so clearly right, I felt quite dim for not having thought of this myself.

Since he was on a roll, I pitched up a question.

'Should I see my mother's behaviour as an attempt to con everyone, or just as a rational response to an awful childhood?'

'Maybe a bit of both,' he replied. 'It may have been reinforced over time. As a young woman, she wanted to be free of where she found herself. Then, after a while, it worked. And the fact it worked would tend to reinforce her satisfaction with it.'

Neil was particularly interested to hear that she may have gone to perhaps a dozen schools. In his clinical practice, he told me, he takes note if people have attended more than about five schools. 'It can create a state of being closed to proper relationships, a lack of confidence in relationships lasting. And there would also have been rumours: "Your father's a crook." Instead she fantasised about a completely different life. Instead of a dad on the run and twelve different schools, she had the big estate and the wealthy parents and the fancy private school.'

So was it common? Had he come across other stories like this in his clinical practice?

'Not really,' he said. 'The more common response to a difficult childhood is to recount it in all its misery, sometimes even to exaggerate the misery, and then say, "Look how far I've come."'

It was the same answer that the genealogical researcher, Nick Barratt, had given me back at the National Archives.

I told Neil the story of her coffin and the grave plot she had all laid out, with the gravestone already engraved and put in place. He didn't seem surprised. 'She has constructed her whole life from birth onwards and so has been constructing her own death. Now that's what I call controlling. I'm very impressed.'

I took another Anzac biscuit. 'So,' I said, 'it's a constructed life.'

Neil nodded. 'It's interesting she was involved in the theatre. That's what plays and books are; they are constructed lives. And that's what she's done; she's created a play. She must have had a magnificent imagination.'

Neil seemed far too won over by the florid subject I'd brought him. So, from the couch, came a little voice.

'But what about me?'

He asked me what I meant, and I talked to him about my need for approval, my hunger to prove myself worthy through my work, and how one bad piece of writing, or one criticism by a listener or reader, will leave me hurt and bruised, as if I'm not worth feeding unless I can write something amusing or agreeable. And yet, I told him, I also possess a crazy-brave confidence. On live radio, in particular, the presenter's ignorance and foolishness is on daily display; you are forced by the medium to begin every sentence not quite knowing where it will end. You can't last five minutes without some level of self-belief.

Neil thought about this for a time. 'You may have inherited some of your mother's anxiety – the sense of "Am I good enough?" But it doesn't sound like your parents were out to get you. They weren't malignant, just neglectful. And for your first three years, you had this substitute mother in New Guinea.'

Neil, as a medical student, had spent some time in New Guinea and fell into a reverie about that country's traditional parenting style – close and physically bonded – and how it creates incredibly confident children. He described walking in the New Guinea Highlands and these groups of children who'd run ahead of the visitors. The kids would stay out for days, sleeping in neighbouring villages, before returning to their own families.

'In those first three years,' he said, 'something was cemented into you, something about confidence and giving. I think that was crucial. You also must have experienced a great loss when you were packed up and removed to Australia. That loss has been swallowed by the fog of infantile amnesia, but it must have been severe.'

Maybe, I thought as I drove away, my mother's story was more upbeat than I thought. She was creative – constructing a series of narratives for herself. The aristocratic only child; then, after she'd run off with Mr Phillipps, the sensualist caught up in the world's most romantic affair. Both of them creations to escape less attractive realities: her father; my father. Yet there was also still a step to go. I needed to properly understand how I was affected, even created, by these inventive narratives; I needed to determine the role I had been allocated in her storylines. The sentiments I'd always expressed to Debra – 'I was never very connected to them'; 'I just wanted to be dutiful' – no longer seemed good enough. In my own ears, they were beginning to sound more like evasions than admissions.

Parenting, PNG style: me with some pals in the New Guinea Highlands.

*

Six months later I was cleaning out my mother's house. I felt guilty doing it. She was always so insistent it be kept in perpetuity, frozen as it was during her reign, all the furniture and books in place, a sort of Presidential Library for Her. We could use it as a holiday house, she'd regularly insisted. In theory, I would have liked to grant my mother's wish, but it didn't seem such a practical idea. She'd long before put me in charge of her legal affairs and, at some point, the house would need to be sold. Dementia had tightened its grip on her: she still seemed to recognise me, but no one else. Sometimes I would talk to her about Mr Phillipps, the great love of her life, hoping to generate a spark of recognition, but even for him there was now not a flicker of response.

I'd flown up on a Friday night after work, hoping I could see my mother twice and clean out her house, all before flying back on Sunday night. It was weird to be there on my own in her silent home. The place was so peculiar, so much an imprint of my mother, with the pool plonked in the centre of the house, the formal English rooms arranged around it, the photo gallery of herself around the walls. I'd ordered packing boxes from the removalist and was dividing things into three categories. The first pile of things would be sent to my son Dan, who had just

267

bought a house in rural Victoria – in the latest town to give him a radio job. Daniel wasn't that keen on receiving a truckload of old furniture, but knowing my mother's horror at her things being sold, I'd encouraged him to at least take a share. The rest I had marked either to Sydney, for sale, or to be carted, by me, into my mother's garage for eventual disposal.

It sounded simple and yet every few minutes I stood frozen – an object in my hand. Was this something valuable or a piece of junk? I didn't really know, I'd just have to decide. At one point, late on the Friday night, I opened a tin trunk and found it stuffed with my mother's clothes from the 1960s – glamorous gowns from designer labels, all dry-cleaned and still in their plastic wrappers. I could get a mint – well, $40 – for these in a second-hand shop in inner Sydney, but did I really want to be bothered?

And then there were things that left me feeling quite tender towards her; in particular, a series of diaries in which she'd written fancy words, presumably dictated by Mr Phillipps, in an attempt to improve her vocabulary, still limited by her interrupted and short-lived schooling.

Carpe diem – seize the day

Mot juste – silent T (Mo)

Fait accompli – deed accomplished

Icarus – Wings with wax, flew too close to sun + fell into sea

Contemporaneous – occurring at the same time

Non-sequitur – conclusion which does not logically follow from
   the premise

Tautology – same thing twice over in different words

Erudite – learned

Slipped into the diaries were little pieces of paper in Mr Phillipps' handwriting, given to her, presumably, in an effort to improve her grammar. A self-appointed Henry Higgins to my mother's Eliza Doolittle, Mr Phillipps had sternly underlined the significant words.

<u>May</u> = Present tense. <u>Might</u> = Past tense. If he <u>left</u> early he <u>might</u> arrive tonight. <u>Observe sequence of tenses.</u>

   <u>Shall</u> & <u>Will</u>

   <u>Singular and Future</u>

   I shall

   You will

   He. She. It will

   <u>Plural</u>

   We shall

   You will

   They will

He then gave examples of the difference between 'will' and 'shall'.

I <u>will</u> be obeyed (equals – I am determined or wish to be.)
You <u>shall</u> be punished (equals – it is decreed.)

I put the notes to one side and contemplated both the lecturing tone and Mr Phillipps' weird, controlling choice of illustrative sentences.

Yes, I know. What a fuckwit.

*

I jumped out of bed early on Saturday morning and decided to tackle the filing cabinet in my mother's office. I'd assumed it would mostly be old tax documents and bank records, easy to discard. I heaved open the first drawer. It was stuffed with papers. I pulled out the first file. It was marked in my mother's handwriting: 'Anna's letters from Canberra to Armidale.' The next said: 'His letters. Stage second.' I delved further into the filing cabinet. It was full of love letters between my mother and Mr Phillipps. Here I was, eight o'clock on a sunny Saturday morning, and it was immediately obvious there were at least hundreds of letters. I soon realised there were thousands.

The correspondence started in 1972. This was only a year after my parents had arrived in Canberra. The affair had started much earlier than I'd imagined. Somehow the Pepys diary stuff now seemed even weirder: presumably Mr Phillipps was already sleeping with my mother, or nearly sleeping with her, while also getting me to record for him every detail of our family life. The letters started as occasional billets-doux, then became weekly, then bi-weekly, then daily, like a speeding-up train. At times, during the white heat of their love affair, they'd exchanged several letters each day and she'd kept them all. My mother had rented a post-office box in Manuka, a Canberra suburb, so she could receive his missives. By early 1974, he was numbering his letters and including both day and time: one would be marked 'No 51. Wednesday evening. 9.30pm.' The next: 'No 52. Wednesday evening. 10.30pm.' Both would be several pages in length.

I sat at my mother's desk, staggered by the sheer size of the collection. Here, in tidy envelopes, was the day-to-day narrative of my mother's love life and the secret, long-term passion that had caused her to leave me and my father. The letters were erotic, there was no getting around that, with much anatomical description. The raunchy language was at its most vivid in his letters to her – with much use of words like 'thrusting' – but reciprocated in her letters to him. They were also romantic, full of Tolkien-inspired whimsy about how they could make a life together, just as soon as my mother was set free of my father. There was talk of stolen afternoons, in which they'd arrange to meet, and of weekends away. It seemed this went on for the best part of three years before she finally left.

She wrote in one letter:

> *I think that our love is terribly special. I sort of know now why God made me wait so long, he knows I am a good girl and he has given me you and I feel he will look after us and let us live long and happily.*

Or again:

> *I love you my Gandalf, love me and know that I shall think of you every moment we are apart, I am yours entirely and yours alone, you found me and made me live and for me there is no other man and there never will be.*

Then, once or twice, the letters become businesslike – my mother recounting the discussions she'd had with a Canberra divorce lawyer.

> *If in any way at all Ted could prove any infidelity on my part he could remove me from the house … if Ted got nasty and did this I could end up with practically nothing and you could be sued for alienation of affection. I explained the rotten marriage I had had and the years and years of drinking and with great difficulty told him of the complete lack of sex.*

In the same letter, she described her dream of living with Mr Phillipps in 'our Hobbit hole' and how she was determined to achieve it by 'having a plan of campaign that is smarter than all the rest can produce'. She ended by saying she had enclosed a cheque, explaining she hoped soon to have more money under her control, at which point she would send more cash. It ended with a lipstick kiss, a real one made by kissing the paper. It was still hot pink after all these years.

After a while, the Manuka post-office box disappeared, and the correspondence shuttled back and forth between Sydney, where my mother had moved temporarily in order to earn money as an arts publicist, and Armidale, where Mr Phillipps had started his employment at the private girls' school.

I flipped though the endless pages – many of the letters two or three thousand words in length – and then spotted a mention of my own name. It was a letter to Mr Phillipps in which my mother recounted how I had telephoned her out of the blue, at 4.30 in the afternoon, without really having anything to say.

She wrote:

I have since felt really bad, wondering about him and what has happened to make him so desperate that he would get home at that time to telephone – I shall never know – I love him – but unbelievably I don't love him not even a part of the amount that I love you.

I sat and read the sentence a few times over. It was hard not to feel hurt by it.

I also noticed that she'd used the term 'my boy' in lots of the letters, which, after a few moments of puzzlement, I realised was her phrase for Mr Phillipps, and not for me, which also produced in me a tiny, surprising stab of pain.

Then in July – I have no memory of this – I visited her in Sydney to mark my sixteenth birthday. My mother wrote to Mr Phillipps the night before my arrival: 'I wish so much you could be here, not even for Rich can I raise one bit of enthusiasm, preparing a party with the most important person absent is just no fun.'

Again, another sharp stab of pain. I thought about the word 'wounded' and how accurate it is to the feeling. I had a self-protective urge to stop reading but it was hard not to glance ahead, to see what happened when I finally arrived to celebrate my birthday. I soon came across the relevant letter: my mother described my birthday party, to which she'd invited some friends of her own and a couple of my old Sydney school friends, whom she described as 'charming'. Next she talked about the 'punishment' of making all the arrangements, before casting ahead to the next day, when I would still be there:

> Don't for a moment think the punishment is finished. I still have to cook a roast and go to the theatre – right at the moment I feel four hundred and six.

So, it was a 'punishment' having me there?

In a letter two days later, after I'd departed, she talked about how I'd bought her a present, a cassette tape which she'd hated. She told Mr Phillipps that she'd already been able to swap it at the local music store.

He bought me a tape of some diabolical group of female singers, I honestly couldn't stand it, so this morning I went to Double Bay early and prevailed on the good man to swap it, I must say it took all my powers of persuasion. In place of the agony, I got Mozart's Violin Concertos K216 and K218 and the Adagio for Violin K261. I chose violin music because I thought it might encourage my very own violinist!

Mr Phillipps, I should note, played the violin.

I mentally skipped through the music I'd loved at the time. A diabolical group of female singers? Yes, that's it: the McGarrigle sisters. I still love them.

There was a final letter dealing with my trip, written a few days later:

Poor Richard. I don't mean to be unkind but it is bliss when it stops, actually it is not the boy's fault this flat is just too small and ill equipped for anyone except you and me, we fit alright but then they could put me in a two foot by six box with you and my world would be right.

'Bliss when it stops.' Even with the Noosa sun streaming in through the windows, this particular phrase seemed a little hard to take – as if my mother was trying to prove her love to Mr Phillipps through a ritual disavowing of her son.

*

The sentence 'My mother never really loved me' is hard to write. I also don't think it's true. I think she loved me intermittently, as best she could. I think she really wanted a child. She went to such effort to achieve that child, it's hard to imagine she wasn't thrilled when I was born. Later on, after Mr Phillipps died, I think she may have loved, or at least needed, me once again.

And, to be honest, I quite like the mix of me. I have a personality in which a rock-solid self-confidence is layered with a bitter, questioning self-contempt. Maybe the combination is easy to explain: I was loved so well and so early in life, but by a substitute, temporary parent – my New Guinea mother, Danota – from whom I was suddenly removed. Danota gave me a crust of confidence, and then later I found Debra, and she reinforced that confidence – even if it remained shot through with self-doubt.

And – maybe this is self-serving – I have respect for both these characteristics: confidence and self-doubt.

To speak up for confidence for a moment: life is like riding a bike. Ride it nervously and it will amplify every miscalculation, throwing the overly anxious to the ground, but ride the bike with bravado and it will shrug off the most egregious of errors. It's the forward propulsion that gives both a bike, and a life, its stability. Ergo: confidence and competence often travel hand in hand.

But here's the difficulty: you also need some fear and self-doubt to ride the bike well. Evolution sensibly built these things into the package. It's fear and self-doubt that told the tribe to post a sentry at night. It's fear and self-doubt that remind us to double-check, to measure twice, to try harder. Fear and self-doubt are the angels of the second draft.

As for me, I'm stupidly confident (witness the radio) and also ridiculously anxious (ask Debra). Like my mother, I always feel the need to prove I am worthy of existence. I check my column five times on a Saturday to see how many people have shared it on Facebook. Every time I hit 'refresh' on the *Sydney Morning Herald* website, I feel poisoned, realising how unhealthy it is to be so anxious about what people think of me. Yet I have a beautiful family: two sons for whom I believe I am a good father, and a partner who has loved me with a protective fierceness since I was twenty-one.

Maybe, in a way, my personality is still formed by my grandfather's criminality and my mother's attempt to escape it, but I'm pretty sure the contagion, to the extent there's a contagion, ends with me. I have snuffed it out. Maybe this is my real life achievement: to snuff out this thing.

My children are both such fine young men. Daniel, now in his mid-twenties, sends me tapes of his radio program. He is hilarious and astute, respectful and warm, with a positive spirit. He loves his listeners and they love him. His program makes the world a better place, which is not always the case with radio. He owns a tumbledown house in the middle of town – a house so cheap that when I went and helped him fit a window lock, a friendly neighbour wandered over and said, 'Mate, don't over-capitalise.'

And Joe, the one with the Vegemite toast and the harmonicas, is now a young architect, his passion for building perhaps ignited by the structures that Debra and I, with our friend Philip, built in the bush. He is hilarious, like his brother, and another positive force in the world, creative and hard-working.

I don't know what to make of the things that made me, but at least – after this strange better-late-than-never quest – I can accurately describe the mix of those things. There was a mother escaping a criminal father; a father who was uninterested but also fairly friendly; there was a loving substitute mother who gave me the gift of her child-centred Papuan culture; and there was an English teacher whose enthusiasm for Pepys was perhaps more self-interested than I understood at the time.

And I have some wonderful cousins – a set ignored, plus a set I didn't even realise existed. Maybe that's the most important outcome of my quest. I now know how important they are.

There's a destructive myth that nearly all parents love their children; that every parent gives their child the unconditional love they deserve. We have a whole language around the inexorability of this love: it's instinctive, we say, before going on to talk about cats with their kittens or cows with their calves. It's built into our very DNA, we say, that a mother loves her children, and so does a father. And yet … Grab a group of your friends at a pub or dinner party and ask them: 'Who feels they were given the love they deserved as a child?' I don't claim all of them will say 'I didn't get that love.' Maybe 60 per cent will say, 'My parents were not perfect, but, yes, they gave me the love that every child deserves.' But I hazard that 40 per cent will say, 'No, now you ask. Not me. I didn't get anything like the love I would hope to give a child of my own.'

Parental love may be instinctive but there are so many barriers to its delivery. There's gambling, or career obsession, or a mum who took too many pills, or a dad who lost his job and became subsumed with bitterness, or a billion other barriers much more bizarre. In my case, if this doesn't sound too grand, perhaps it was the British class system and my mother's efforts to escape it, together with my father's drinking and their shared narcissism.

It doesn't take much to create a barrier between the instinct and the act. Yet here's what I find interesting: so many people had inadequate childhoods but we're not all insane or self-harming or miserable. We just found the love we needed elsewhere. For me, it was Danota. Later: Canberra Youth Theatre, Steve Stephens, my partner Debra, her parents Max and Teresa, my boys.

This is the amazing resilience of humans. We are hungry for love and – mostly – we somehow find it.

Like all the players of Who's Got the Weirdest Parents?, I'm left with wounds, dealt out in childhood and mostly overcome.

They are still wounds, of course, but just flesh wounds.

Acknowledgements

The leaping-off point for this story was a piece I wrote for *Good Weekend*, so thanks to the editor, Ben Naparstek. Odd hints of the story have also appeared in some of my other books: the Vegemite story, from *In Bed with Jocasta*, was too germane not to include.

The events are as I remember them, although others may recall them differently. I've tried to capture the rhythm and meaning of the conversations, although the exact words are my best effort. Like most people, I didn't take contemporaneous shorthand notes, although some lines – 'The natives did it' – burn themselves into the mind with an intensity that allows me to claim them as word-for-word accurate.

Thanks to my friends who battled through an early version of the manuscript and helped me fashion the tale: Kate Holden, Philip Clark, Jenny McAsey and Michael Robotham. I also owe a debt of gratitude to the British writer Jeanette Winterson who kindly read an early draft – proof that loyalty runs deep in people with a link to Accrington.

In terms of researching the background history, thanks to both Dr Robert Lyneham and Professor Kara Swanson for helping me understand what birth via artificial insemination might have meant in 1958. Professor Swanson's spiky journal article, from which I've quoted, is titled 'Adultery by Doctor: Artificial Insemination, 1890–1945'.

The detail about life in 1950s Port Moresby largely comes from Ian Stuart's history *Port Moresby Yesterday and Today* and from Jim Huxley's memoir *New Guinea Experience*. For Florence Broadhurst, I relied on Helen O'Neill's much-lauded biography.

Amruta Slee from HarperCollins provided the best possible notes: demanding and insistent when things could be better; warm and encouraging when something happened to work. Any shortcomings in the manuscript are surely her fault, since I did nearly everything she suggested. My gratitude also to Amanda O'Connell for her copy editing.

Thanks most of all to my partner, Debra Oswald, for encouraging me, over many years, to write this. I'd been so fierce about limiting my mother and father's sway over my life that I felt reluctant about spending a couple of years writing a book about a relationship which I'd so assiduously tried to slough aside. Then again, as Debra strenuously argued, the story is intriguing and,

I hope, useful to other contestants in that world-wide game Who's Got the Weirdest Parents?. She helped create this book. And she rescued me.

I should also thank her for a lifetime of correcting my spelling. Mind you, if my mother hadn't run off with my English teacher …

George Clooney's Haircut

Richard Glover's skewed stories of everyday life depict a world both weird and wry – in which Henry VIII provides marriage advice, JD Salinger celebrates tap water and naked French women bring forth a medical miracle. It's also a world in which shampoo is eschewed, the second-rate is praised and George Clooney's haircut can help save a relationship.

Bizarre yet commonplace, absurd yet warm-hearted, these stories will expose the true strangeness of the life you are living right now.

Why Men Are Necessary

Wickedly funny stories of everyday life, as heard on ABC Radio's *Thank God It's Friday*. Salute the sexy and feisty Jocasta; confront teenage rebellion in the form of a fish called Wanda; do battle with magpies the size of small fighter jets; try to work out which font you use when speaking the language of love; and find out what men really have to offer.

In Richard Glover's stories, the day-to-day becomes vivid, magical and laugh-out-loud funny.

Desperate Husbands

Revisit Richard, the original desperate husband, and his partner, the fabulous but formidable Jocasta. And say hello to their teenage offspring – the Teutonic Batboy and his irrepressible younger brother, The Space Cadet. *Desperate Husbands* lifts the lid on so-called normal family life, and reveals its soulful, hilarious absurdity. Welcome to a world where household appliances conspire against their owners, fathers practise ballet in the hallway, and dead insects spell out an SOS on the kitchen floor.